FISHING SMALL FLIES

Joel -
Good luck fishing -
the small flies

Ed Engle

STACKPOLE
BOOKS

Published by
STACKPOLE BOOKS
5067 Ritter Road
Mechanicsburg, PA 17055
www.stackpolebooks.com

Printed in the United States

First edition

10 9 8 7 6 5 4 3 2 1

Illustrations by Dave Hall and Caroline Stover.
Photos by the author.

Library of Congress Cataloging-in-Publication Data
Engle, Ed, 1950-
  Fishing small flies / Ed Engle.—1st ed.
      p. cm.
  Includes bibliographical references and index.
  ISBN 0-8117-0124-7 (hardcover)
  1. Fly fishing. I. Title.
SH456.E56 2004
799.12'4—dc22

2004009145

CONTENTS

FOREWORD

The last time I fished with Ed Engle we were out in a johnboat on a weedy 800-acre lake. I was at the oars and Ed was standing in the bow, deftly plucking largemouth bass from potholes in the thick bulrushes. He was using a rig that most small-fly trout fishers would think of as a rug beater: a nine-foot, 8-weight rod, a 30-pound leader, and a five-inch-long rabbit fur streamer. During the inevitable slow spells, he was talking about an upcoming return trip to Alaska for king salmon where the rods would be two sizes heavier and the fish even bigger.

If that doesn't seem to have a lot of bearing on a book about fishing small flies, consider that a good fisherman is a good fisherman, regardless of the quarry or the size of the hooks, and that flippin' for bass in thick cover is not entirely unlike short line nymphing for trout with a size 22 midge pupa, although with bass you do want to set the hook a bit harder.

The fact is, there are more similarities than differences between types of fishing, and a well-rounded angler like Ed tends to have a more eclectic view of things than a myopic specialist. He can translate tactics and approaches from one species or water type to another because, in the long run, they're all just fish and we're all just fishermen.

But of course Ed does qualify as a small-fly specialist because he's done a lot of small-fly fishing for a very long time. He's successfully fished miniature flies for decades for difficult trout in sometimes inscrutable spring creeks and tailwaters, both as a fisherman and as a guide, where he not only has to know the techniques inside out, but also has to be able to explain them succinctly to excited or despondent fishermen. That takes the kind of self-awareness that allows you to know exactly what you're doing and why you're doing it. It also takes the facility with plain-spoken language that keeps your descriptions from sounding like technical gibberish. That combination is rare among guides and writers, but Ed has it, both on the water and on the page.

Those of you who are familiar with Ed's work will recognize this as a companion volume to his previous book, *Tying Small Flies*. He wrote both out of a characteristic sense of completeness and followed the book on fly patterns with this one because, as important as fly patterns can be, there's still a lot more to catching fish than just having the right fly, even to the point that it's better to fish the wrong fly well than to fish the right one poorly.

He's done a fine job of it. Both books stand on their own, with virtually no repetition between them. You can read one or the other or both in no particular order, but together they comprise a magnum opus on the subject.

As always, Ed's advice is like his fishing: informed, well considered, and with no wasted motion. His crystal clear explanation of how tailwaters and spring creeks work is alone worth the price of admission. The same goes for his tip on how to try speed casting with the rod you already have instead of buying a specialized new stick just for that purpose.

He's also an advocate of simplicity in a sport that has gotten increasingly complicated. It may be true—as it was with me—that you won't realize you don't need everything until you've owned and used everything at least once, but I suggest you listen to Ed when he tells you to pare down the gear in order to put as little as possible between you and the fish. He's right, and it's hard-earned wisdom.

I also like Ed's sense of practicality, as in his advice about choosing tackle. There may be no such thing as perfect fly tackle (not that that keeps any of us from looking) but Ed suggests that you at least get stuff that won't detract from the fishing.

I especially liked his discussion of how to see fish: one of the most useful things a fisherman can learn to do. I know Ed to be an excellent fish spotter. He sees them when I don't, and when I see two, he sees six. He says it comes from guiding, and it probably does, although you can't completely rule out natural talent. Anyway, what he says about spotting fish is worth some study and practice. You may never get as good at it as Ed is, but it *is* possible to train yourself to see more than you do now.

Ed even delves a little into the imponderables: the instinct or fish sense that separates the good fishermen from the precious few great ones. This can be heady stuff. It's undeniably real, but many writers aren't aware of it and many others are afraid to touch it. My advice is give it a chance, even if your mind doesn't automatically work that way.

Like most of the best fishermen, Ed's skills aren't always obvious when he's fishing. He usu-ally doesn't seem to be doing anything differently than any other fisherman on the river—except that he's often catching more fish. That's because he can not only spot fish, but observation and experience tell him where to look. His cast may look like anyone else's, but it's more likely to be right over a trout and also more likely to be with the right type of fly, since the fish's behavior tells him what it's feeding on and where—right on the surface, in the film, an inch deep, six inches. . . .

And things just always seem to go smoothly for no apparent reason. Some of that comes from a lifetime on the water, but there's also an attention to small, but sometimes crucial, details. For instance, Ed always keeps his line wound neatly and snugly on the reel. Even on a good day, you may not get a fish that takes much line, but you never know when you'll hook a screamer and when it happens you don't want a rat's nest in your reel.

When it comes right down to it, this is the kind of fishing book we all look for and too seldom find: the one written by an experienced fisherman who knows how to catch fish and who's a good enough writer to let us in on how he does it.

John Gierach

INTRODUCTION

A few years ago when I was writing *Tying Small Flies,* I knew that I wasn't telling the whole story. As much as I liked tying and designing small flies, I understood that having the right tiny fly imitation wasn't all there was to catching a trout. I even found myself making allusions to the importance of small-fly fishing technique in the book. It was clear to me then that I had a lot more to say about how to fish small flies.

Fishing Small Flies is the product of many years of fishing small flies mostly on western rivers and spring creeks but also on some of the storied eastern and southern small-fly waters. Most of what I have to say concerns how you can refine and, in some cases, modify basic fly-fishing techniques to accommodate the unique challenges of fishing small flies. I've organized the book to provide a foundation that includes definitions of classic small-fly water and some other less common small-fly fishing opportunities. I've taken a look at tackle and various other odds and ends that are useful to small-fly anglers.

There is a special emphasis placed on making observations of trout that are feeding on small flies. One of the great pleasures of fishing small flies is that the trout are often feeding in shallow, clear water. The best fishing revolves around spotting and carefully stalking a single trout. Making insightful observations and then acting on those observations are the basis of successful small-fly angling.

I've included chapters on basic subsurface small-fly techniques and fishing small flies on and near the surface. I consider these chapters, coupled with the one on striking, landing, and playing trout on small flies, as the real foundation for fishing small flies. Developing these skills to the point where they are instinctive paves the way to fishing small flies at the highest level.

All of the chapters in the book should act as building blocks to the chapter on fishing the major small-fly hatches. I pay special attention to the hatches I am most familiar with as a western small-fly fisher, but I know that much of the information can be translated to specific hatches in other parts of the country. An even more crucial idea included in the chapter is that it's possible to match more than the hatch. When you fish small flies it's important to use every observation at your disposal. This may mean that in some fishing situations it becomes most important to match the riseform rather than the hatch. In another scenario it may be crucial to match your cast to a riseform.

In an effort to go beyond matching the hatch I've expanded standard hatch charts to include matching small-fly pattern types to riseforms and other observations that fly fishers normally make. Hopefully, the charts will provide a starting point for a more comprehensive on-the-water process for catching trout on the small fly. None of this is new. It's more about making out-of-the-ordinary connections between familiar fly-fishing tactics—maybe a certain cast works better at the beginning of a hatch than at the end, or what happens if we take special care to match a small-fly pattern to a specific riseform rather than an insect?

Finally, you'll find a thread running through this book about less being more. I think that the best fly fishing occurs when there's as little between me and the trout as possible. It seems only natural that the ultimate goal of fishing small flies should be lightness. If I can catch a trout on a single size 24 fly attached to a 6X or 7X leader fished on a sensitive, well-tuned fly rod, it makes my day. But I now acknowledge that there can be another level to the experience. I think that beyond the fly-fishing fundamentals, beyond the tackle, and beyond the fly patterns, fishing small flies will hone your instincts to a fine edge. That's when it comes down to the only thing between you and the trout—a cobweb-thin tippet.

There are always other fly fishers, writers, editors, and publishers to thank when you write a fly-fishing book. Several chapters in this book appeared in different shorter versions in *American Angler* magazine and *Flyfishing & Tying Journal*. Art Scheck, John Likakis, Dave Hughes, Kim Koch, and Phil Monahan have all had a hand at editing and improving my articles over the years. John Randolph at *Fly Fisherman* magazine provided important input on striking and hooking fish. Entomologist/fly fisher Rick Hafele made significant contributions to this book concerning small-fly entomology and life cycles. Judith Schnell and Amy Lerner at Stackpole Books direct the process where all the pieces are fitted together so nicely into a book.

None of this could happen without time on the river, and it doesn't hurt to fish with talented and insightful fly fishers such as Gary Anderson, A. K. Best, John Gierach, Roy Palm, Stan Benton, Mike Clark, Roger Hill, Gary Willmart, Dusty Sprague, and Peter Kummerfeldt. I should also thank all of the people I've guided on Colorado's South Platte River over the past fifteen years. It is a great small-fly river, and by guiding all of you I've really learned how to see trout. The opportunity to just observe trout day in and day out has, more than anything else, taught me how to fish small flies.

Dan Wecks at the Business of Art Center in Manitou Springs, Colorado, provided a quiet, pleasant workplace to write and edit this book. Dave Woverton provided technical support for the photography. Dusty Sprague, a Federation of Fly Fishers Certified Master Casting Instructor, demonstrated the casts that I photographed for this book and added insight into the nature of what makes a fishing cast work.

I'm sure I've left a few names out of these acknowledgments. If one of them is yours, please accept my thanks for your contributions.

Finally, thanks to my sweetheart Jana Rush, who has always found the time to run up to the river with me when I needed someone to help me take one last photo. My mother, Bernice Engle, and sister, Carolyn Reyes, as always are there to support me when the going gets tough.

My thanks, again.

CHAPTER ONE

Anatomy of a Small-Fly River

The wild irises are in full bloom along Colorado's South Platte River. As much as I admire the vibrant color they bring to the valley floor, I must confess that my appreciation goes beyond the flower's beauty. Each year when the iris are in bloom the river comes alive with a convergence of aquatic insect hatches that bring even the shy, oversize brown trout to the surface.

I like to be on the water at dawn when the robust-bodied little mayflies the fly fishermen call *Tricos* hatch. Or more accurately, I should say when the *female* Tricos hatch and are then followed into the air by the males, who hatched at twilight the night before and have been patiently awaiting the arrival of the females. The newly emerged females that successfully make it into the air go directly into mating swarms. A portion of those who don't are consumed by trout that have queued up in the feeding lanes, also awaiting the females' arrival. Needless to say, those rising trout are the reason for my early arrival to the river. They often supply the least difficult Trico angling of the day.

Somewhere toward the end of the Trico hatch a smattering of small, tan caddisflies begins to pop from the surface. The hatch doesn't present the abundance of insects that the Tricos do, but nonetheless it is a predictable yearly event and the trout make up for the lack of naturals by exuberantly chasing down every one they can. With time on this river, during these sweet weeks, you learn that a little CDC caddis imitation fished *before* you see any naturals on the water will often be greeted by the splashy rise of a very nice size trout.

As the caddisflies continue to trickle off the water, you will begin to see the great mating swarms of Tricos hovering closer and closer to the water's surface. The first of the Trico females that fall spent to the water's surface after laying eggs will be met by the nonchalant sipping rises of the trout that are now stacked into the feeding lanes. A little run that might have held a fish or two is suddenly clogged with ten or fifteen fish patiently sipping the spent spinners. Before long the surface is thick with spinners and rising trout. Then there is a lull, followed by another pulse of rises in response to another raft of spent spinners drifting downstream on the water's surface.

A well-presented imitation will catch trout. This is the very beginning of a hatch and spinner fall that will last four months. Right now the trout are intoxicated with the easy pickings. In a week the largest trout will be feeding almost exclusively on drowned spent spinners. The other trout will have become more discriminating. In a month it will take everything you know about fishing small flies to get a fish to take. But for now, the fishing is sweet.

Somewhere in the thick of the spinner fall, you'll catch a glimpse of a lighter, pale yellow mayfly. If it's on the surface, there is a good chance you'll see a riseform quite unlike the sipping Trico rise. The rise will have the authority of a trout who knows whatever it is after might get away. These are hatching pale morning duns that are imbedded in the Trico spinner fall this time of year. The trout will go out of their way to take them, often to the extent of completely ignoring the Trico spinners.

Sometime between noon and two in the afternoon, what began with the female Trico hatch and progressed to include a caddisfly hatch that eventually led to a pale morning dun hatch will end as the last of the Tricos fall spent to the water's surface. The trout that are stacked in the feeding lanes disappear.

The first questions that an observant fly fisher new to the South Platte River will ask are what accounts for this great abundance of aquatic insects and why are most of them so small?

TAILWATERS

Okay, there's a hook to the story. The section of the South Platte River I was describing is a tailwater. It's the regulated river that occurs below the dam on the Spinney Mountain Reservoir. This particular reservoir, like five others on the South Platte, is a water storage reservoir that serves the Denver metropolitan area and agricultural users on Colorado's high arid plains. Engineers use the reservoirs to store the water. The river is then used to transport it downstream. Reservoirs operated solely to generate electricity are less common in the western states, but they do account for some legendary tailwater fishing in Arkansas, Missouri, Kentucky, and Tennessee. Some reservoirs like the Flaming Gorge Reservoir on the Green River in Utah are used to store water *and* generate electricity on the side.

The tailwaters that occur below water storage reservoirs in temperate climate zones are the most

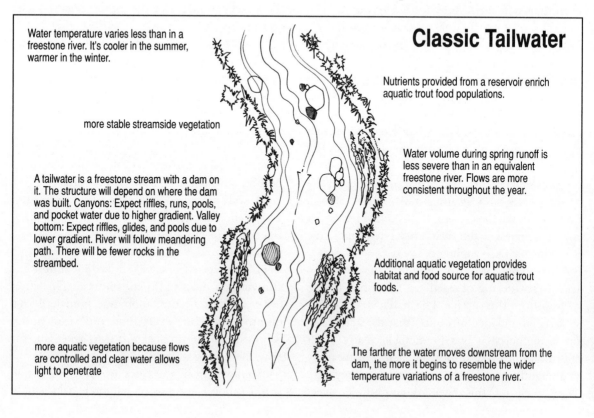

Water temperature varies less than in a freestone river. It's cooler in the summer, warmer in the winter.

more stable streamside vegetation

A tailwater is a freestone stream with a dam on it. The structure will depend on where the dam was built. Canyons: Expect riffles, runs, pools, and pocket water due to higher gradient. Valley bottom: Expect riffles, glides, and pools due to lower gradient. River will follow meandering path. There will be fewer rocks in the streambed.

more aquatic vegetation because flows are controlled and clear water allows light to penetrate

Classic Tailwater

Nutrients provided from a reservoir enrich aquatic trout food populations.

Water volume during spring runoff is less severe than in an equivalent freestone river. Flows are more consistent throughout the year.

Additional aquatic vegetation provides habitat and food source for aquatic trout foods.

The farther the water moves downstream from the dam, the more it begins to resemble the wider temperature variations of a freestone river.

Tailwaters still look like the freestone rivers they once were, but their trout-growing potential rivals that of a spring creek.

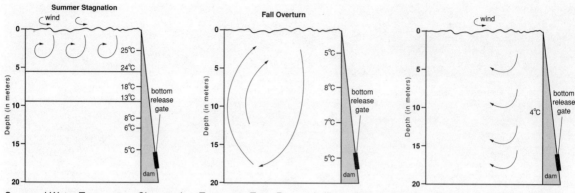

Seasonal Water Temperature Changes in a Temperate Zone Reservoir *Illustrations derived from* Biology, *3rd ed., by Helena Curtis, p. 891. Top left:* In summer the top layer of water (epilimnion) is warmed when the wind mixes it with warm air temperatures. The less dense, warmer water stays on top. Water temperatures drop quickly in the middle layer (thermocline). A bottom layer of water (hypolimnion) is the coldest. *Top middle:* In autumn the upper layer of water is cooled when the wind mixes it with cooler air temperatures. The temperature of the epilimnion cools to that of the hypolimnion and the water in the entire reservoir circulates, causing the fall overturn. *Top right:* Eventually the entire reservoir reaches the same temperature.

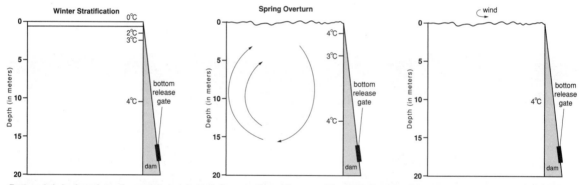

Bottom left: In the winter the surface cools to 0 degrees C and freezes. The less dense, coldest water remains near the surface and the warmer water remains near the bottom. Winter stratification then occurs. *Bottom middle:* In spring the ice melts and once again the wind mixes the surface with warm air temperatures. The water in the entire reservoir then circulates and the spring overturn occurs. *Bottom right:* Eventually the entire reservoir reaches the same temperature. Warming air temperatures then set the stage once again for summer stagnation. This seasonal cycle of water temperatures in temperate-zone reservoirs with bottom release gates results in cooler water temperatures in the summer and warmer water temperatures in the winter in the tailwater below the reservoir.

important to small–fly enthusiasts. Many of the older reservoirs have the gates near the bottom of the dam. If you are familiar with lakes and reservoirs in temperate climates, you'll know that the water stratifies into layers with different temperatures during the summer. The warmest water (epilimnion) is on the surface because the wind is constantly mixing it with the warmer air temperatures. The next layer, known as the thermocline, is where water temperatures rapidly decrease. The bottom layer of water (hypolimnion) is the coldest.

As autumn approaches, the air temperature gets colder and colder. The wind continues to mix it with the epilimnion, but the result now is

Tailwaters located in valleys where the gradient is low resemble spring creeks in their appearance and ability to produce trout.

that it cools the water until it eventually reaches the temperature of the thermocline and ultimately the cold temperatures of the hypolimnion. This results in the fall turnover when, for a period of time, the water temperature is the same from top to bottom in the reservoir.

As the air temperatures get colder and colder, water does a weird thing. It becomes *less* dense. When ice forms on the reservoir's surface the coldest layer of water is on top. The bottom layer of water that's still liquid is warmer. It stays like that until spring when the air temperature and solar radiation combine to melt the ice. What is now colder, denser water tends to sink to the bottom, while all the time the warm spring winds are mixing with, and warming, the upper layers of water. This results in the spring turnover when once again water temperatures throughout

the reservoir are the same. But before long the water begins to stratify by temperature again, summer arrives, and we're back where we started.

By now you're probably thinking, "Who cares!" But hang on. If you like fishing small flies, you will care. Here's the point. Because the gates on many dams are bottom-release, you get a temperature effect in tailwaters known as "summer cool–winter warm." It means that in the wintertime the somewhat warmer water from the bottom of the reservoir is being released into the tailwater. That's why the river doesn't freeze up so much right below the dam and, depending on the flows, for several miles downstream of it. The warmer water is why tailwater trout are more active in winter. Conversely, in the summer the water being drawn from the bottom layer of the reservoir is a bit cooler. So in the summer a

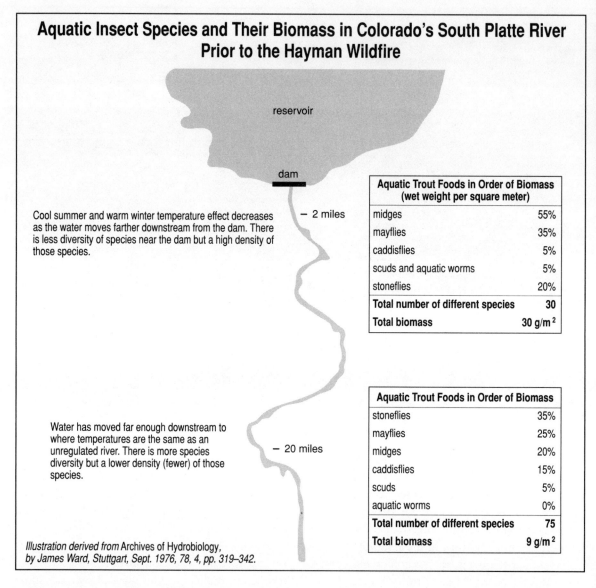

Aquatic Insect Species and Their Biomass in Colorado's South Platte River Prior to the Hayman Wildfire

reservoir

dam

— 2 miles

Cool summer and warm winter temperature effect decreases as the water moves farther downstream from the dam. There is less diversity of species near the dam but a high density of those species.

Aquatic Trout Foods in Order of Biomass (wet weight per square meter)	
midges	55%
mayflies	35%
caddisflies	5%
scuds and aquatic worms	5%
stoneflies	20%
Total number of different species	**30**
Total biomass	**30 g/m²**

Water has moved far enough downstream to where temperatures are the same as an unregulated river. There is more species diversity but a lower density (fewer) of those species.

— 20 miles

Aquatic Trout Foods in Order of Biomass	
stoneflies	35%
mayflies	25%
midges	20%
caddisflies	15%
scuds	5%
aquatic worms	0%
Total number of different species	**75**
Total biomass	**9 g/m²**

Illustration derived from Archives of Hydrobiology, *by James Ward, Stuttgart, Sept. 1976, 78, 4, pp. 319–342.*

tailwater has a bit cooler water temperature than an equivalent unregulated river would have.

Overall this means that a tailwater has a *narrower* range of water temperatures over the course of a year than an equivalent unregulated river. That's important when it comes to the aquatic insects and other aquatic food sources that trout like to eat because some insect groups found in unregulated rivers require a broader range of temperatures to develop. It's the reason

you're not going to see the giant stonefly species up near the dam in most tailwaters or certain species of caddisflies or many of the larger mayflies. They all need the broader range of temperature cues to thrive.

What you will find are species of aquatic insects that are suited to this more narrow range of water temperatures. And you guessed it—these tend to be the smaller species of mayflies such as blue-winged olives, Tricos, and pale morning duns. The tiny two-winged flies of the order Diptera that fly fishermen call midges are the big winners in the tailwater environment. They often occur in astronomical numbers.

There's actually *less* aquatic insect species diversity in the tailwater. This isn't necessarily good news from an ecological point of view because diversity means stability, but on the other hand, the species that can live in the tailwater environment do more than just get by—they thrive. From a trout's point of view that means breakfast, lunch, dinner, hors d'oeuvres, snacks, and bedtime treats are on the table. Some tailwaters are such rich environments that trout will average an inch of growth a month.

Needless to say, the farther you move downstream from the dam the more the tailwater will begin to resemble an unregulated freestone stream. The overall density of aquatic insects will go down as the nutrients supplied from the reservoir diminish and the water temperatures begin to fluctuate through a broader range, but the diversity of species will increase.

Trout may become quite selective due to the lack of diversity in tailwater aquatic insect populations. The abundance of food created in the nutrient-rich tailwater means the trout don't have to feed opportunistically on any old thing that floats downstream just to be sure they'll make it through the winter. In addition, they don't have to identify a lot of different species of insects as food sources. They can concentrate on the few, but plentiful tailwater species they are familiar with.

The only down side to the summer cool–winter warm scenario is that in some especially deep reservoirs the water released may be *so* cold or so lacking in nutrients that it inhibits aquatic insect growth and falls below the temperature range needed for optimal trout growth. It's easy to identify these tailwaters because trout populations are thin right below the dam but increase farther downstream where the water tempera-

tures are a bit warmer. This problem has been overcome in some newer dams by placing gates on the dam at different water depths, which allow engineers to mix water temperatures or add some nutrient-rich water from the thermocline to create a better habitat for trout in the tailwater.

The way a reservoir's water is released also has an impact on the river below. In a typical small-fly tailwater below a storage reservoir the water flows are altered in accordance with downstream needs. Although to anglers it may seem like those flows bounce up and down quite a bit, the fluctuations are actually more stable than in an unregulated river where spring runoff from nearby mountains can dramatically increase the water volume and muddy it for months. In the summer, thunderstorms may again muddy the river off and on for a few days at a time.

The controlled water releases also result in more stable streambanks, which mean even less turbidity in the water. This explains the year-round water clarity found in tailwaters except when runoff from an unregulated tributary stream that enters below the dam temporarily muddies it. The streambed isn't scoured out by high-volume spring runoff, either. Although insect species that need "clean" rubble may suffer, species that aren't affected by the additional silts will thrive. In addition, the year-round clear water allows sunlight to penetrate the water. The result is aquatic vegetation that remains stable, and since the spring runoff is controlled, the plants aren't scoured out each spring, although especially heavy releases of water may occasionally disrupt them. The aquatic vegetation provides habitat for important noninsect trout foods such as microscuds and some species of mayflies.

Nutrient levels are also higher in tailwaters because the reservoir acts like a giant solar collector storing energy from the sun in animal and plant life. That energy is eventually converted into nutrients in the water that are then released into the tailwater below, providing a plentiful food base for aquatic insects. In the Rocky Mountains, many tailwaters are naturally alkaline. This is a more productive environment for aquatic insects than acid waters.

Colorado's South Park is an example of a lime-rich intermountain valley. As the South Platte meanders through it, numerous rich alkaline tributaries flow into the river, producing ideal water chemistry for trout. Couple this with the reservoir's nutrient creating potential, the water temperature consistency provided by the summer cool–winter warm effect, and more stable water flows and the tailwater becomes a trout factory. It's as close as you can get to a man-made replica of nature's greatest trout factory of all—a spring creek.

SPRING CREEKS

The first time I seriously fished spring creeks was in Paradise Valley, Montana. John Gierach and I were in a road trip mood, and we decided to head to Montana from Colorado. This was long enough ago that neither one of us was making a lot of money, and more importantly, neither one of us cared much about making a lot of money. That meant we both had time on our hands. And time meant open-ended, meandering road trips through trout country with thrifty, no frills, under-the-stars-every-night fishing camps.

We drifted toward the Jefferson River, stopping at Three Dollar Bridge on the Madison, dropping into Willow Creek, the Gallatin, the Boulder, and, yes, the spring creeks of Paradise Valley. I'd been waiting my whole life to fish spring creeks. I knew they wouldn't be exactly like my home river, the South Platte tailwater, but I had heard that spring-creek trout favored small flies, were often selective, and got *big*. All of which was familiar to me from my days on the South Platte. I was anxious to see if I could apply my tailwater knowledge to a spring creek.

Nelson's Spring Creek took my breath away. The morning we arrived was dead calm. The water loafed across the valley floor. There were long stretches where the near flawless surface was marred by only a feathery seam, momentary undulation, or gentle push of current. The swaying aquatic vegetation under the surface was often the only indication that the water was moving at all. Perfectly clear water revealed trout neatly lined up in the feeding lanes. They gracefully dipped and turned, picking nymphs from the water. Occasionally, one drifted back with the current and tipped its head up and plucked something small from the water's surface.

My trance was later broken as we watched a pale morning dun lazily drifting downstream until it disappeared into a ring on the water's surface. Other duns followed. We pulled out our fly boxes. We were in business.

Nelson's is the classic spring creek. Unlike a man-made tailwater where a surface reservoir supplies a reasonably consistent source of water, spring creeks well up from underground reservoirs known as aquifers. They are most commonly associated with geothermal basins, limestone marl bogs, geyser basins, porous volcanic rock, and river valleys where the water percolates down through the streambed rubble and emerges somewhere else above the ground as a spring creek. Spring creeks are characterized by their constant flows and consistent temperatures.

The classic spring creeks you read about in fly-fishing literature meander through a low gradient valley or meadow where streambed rocks and boulders are uncommon. This explains the water's uncommonly smooth surface. It's also one of the differences between a spring creek and a tailwater. Tailwaters, which were freestone rivers or creeks at some point in their lives, usually retain the structure of their previous incarnation. That means there are pools, riffles, runs, and glides. But don't make the mistake of thinking

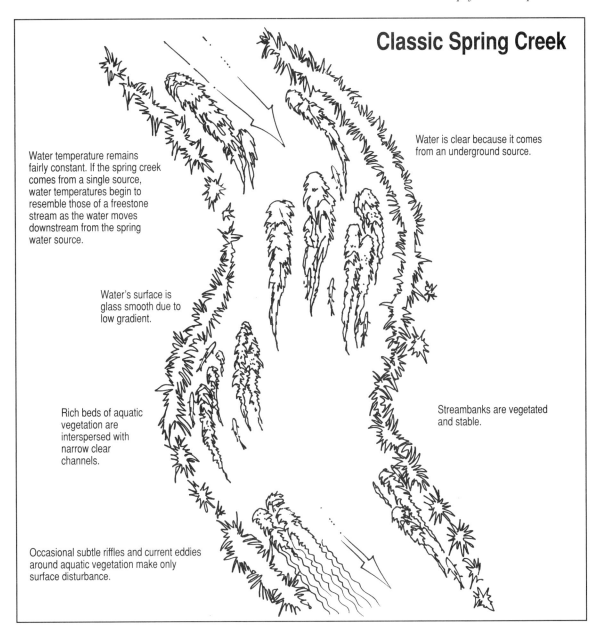

Classic Spring Creek

Water temperature remains fairly constant. If the spring creek comes from a single source, water temperatures begin to resemble those of a freestone stream as the water moves downstream from the spring water source.

Water is clear because it comes from an underground source.

Water's surface is glass smooth due to low gradient.

Rich beds of aquatic vegetation are interspersed with narrow clear channels.

Streambanks are vegetated and stable.

Occasional subtle riffles and current eddies around aquatic vegetation make only surface disturbance.

that *all* spring creeks are classic spring creeks. Consider some sections of the Henry's Fork in Idaho, where there are so many runs and riffles that you'd be hard pressed to believe it's a spring creek at all . . . until you see it around Last Chance, where it's as serene as any chalkstream that Frederick Halford fished in southern England.

The similarities between tailwaters and spring creeks are significant, though. Take your favorite tailwater, kick it up a few notches, and you have your favorite spring creek. The somewhat stable flows that characterize storage-reservoir water releases are considerably more stable in a spring creek, although they will sometimes vary de-

Classic spring creeks are often found in valleys where the gradient is low. They are characterized by clear, slow moving waters with few instream rocks.

pending on local rainfall. The narrow range of water temperatures found in bottom-release storage-reservoir tailwaters is sometimes even narrower in spring creeks where water temperatures may vary by only a few degrees.

Mike Lawson states in *Spring Creeks* that the temperature at the source in the most productive spring creeks is 50 to 58 degrees F. This falls very close to a trout's preferred temperature range. Since the spring creek stays close to those temperatures year-round, it means the trout stay active and grow year-round. And we all know what that means.

The water clarity that characterizes a tailwater is also present in a spring creek, and the nutrient-rich, alkaline water often associated with Rocky Mountain tailwaters is the rule rather than the exception for most spring creeks. In addition, the water clarity, stable flows, and nutrient-rich water produce abundant aquatic vegetation, which provides habitat for other aquatic trout foods and hiding cover for young trout.

The narrow range of water temperatures and the highly productive water chemistry in spring creeks impact the aquatic insect life in much the same way as in tailwaters. Overall, fewer species of aquatic insects will thrive in spring creeks, but those species that do often occur in huge numbers. Most of them are smaller sized.

A final similarity between spring creeks and tailwaters is that the farther you move from the source, whether it's a dam or where the spring water wells up to the surface, the more they begin to resemble a freestone stream. The one exception for spring creeks is when they occur in an area that is rich in springs that continue to charge the creek as it meanders downstream, preserving its unique characteristics.

When I started fishing spring creeks, I was able to transfer much of my tailwater knowledge of small flies and how to fish them directly to spring creek fishing situations. The flat, smooth water common on many spring creeks did force me to pay more attention to my presentations, though. Over the years I've also come to believe that hatches are more numerous and last longer on spring creeks than they are on tailwaters. That means that small dry-fly and emerger fishing techniques may be more important on spring creeks than on tailwaters where small-fly nymphing tactics and finesse are crucial. Finally, when compared with tailwaters, I've found a bit more aquatic insect species diversity on many of the spring creeks I've fished. That diversity sometimes includes a few larger sized insects.

I wish that we would all be so lucky as to have a spring creek in our backyard or at least within easy driving distance of home. I can't think of a more fascinating place to fish small flies, but if you don't have a neighborhood spring creek, a tailwater below a water storage reservoir is a good second choice. Almost everything you learn on a tailwater you'll be able to apply to a spring creek when you do get a chance to fish one.

FREESTONE STREAMS

In 1977 I had a one-room cabin on the Arkansas River near Salida, Colorado. The Arkansas is what we call a caddis river in the Rockies. Most caddis rivers are characterized by at least one annual blizzard hatch. In the case of the Arkansas River, it's the Mother's Day caddisfly hatch that in a good year comes well before the runoff in April.

At the peak of the hatch, there are so many size 14 tan caddisflies in the air that you must cover your mouth and nose with a bandana to avoid inhaling four or five caddis with every breath. Needless to say, the trout go nuts when the caddis first start coming off in the morning and until they are so full they can't eat more. Sometimes the best fishing occurs after the morning gorging when the females come back to lay eggs just before dark. Even when the great hatch is over, caddisflies still sporadically come off the river for most of the season. It's a river where an Elk Hair Caddisfly or Stimulator is *always* a productive pattern.

That many caddisflies on any Rocky Mountain river means to me that it's probably a freestone. I've seen some pretty good caddisfly hatches on tailwaters and spring creeks, but nothing like the blizzard hatches on some of the freestones. The big golden stoneflies that are important to fly fishers before and even during the caddisfly hatch on the Arkansas also indicate freestoner to me. You'll see some mayfly hatches, too, as the season progresses, but they seldom make the trout very selective. A Royal Coachman, H & L Variant, Wulff, Stimulator, or in the words of my friend and long-time Arkansas River fly fisher, Clyde Tullis, "anything big and bushy" will usually suffice.

The only thing that keeps the Arkansas from being a classic western freestone river is that there are dams on a few of its tributaries. Water releases from those dams are transported down the Arkansas to the farmers on the eastern plains, but other than evidence of reduced growth rates in the trout due to higher water volumes, the river acts much like any other freestone stream. There is a greater range of water temperatures than in most tailwaters or spring creeks that provide niches for a greater variety of aquatic insect life. But those niches are also more narrow, which means the numbers of any one species (other than the caddisflies!) are not great. The aquatic vegetation in the river is limited because it gets scoured out every spring by the runoff, and the roily water produced by the runoff doesn't allow as much photosynthesis-producing

Freestone Streams in Mountainous Areas

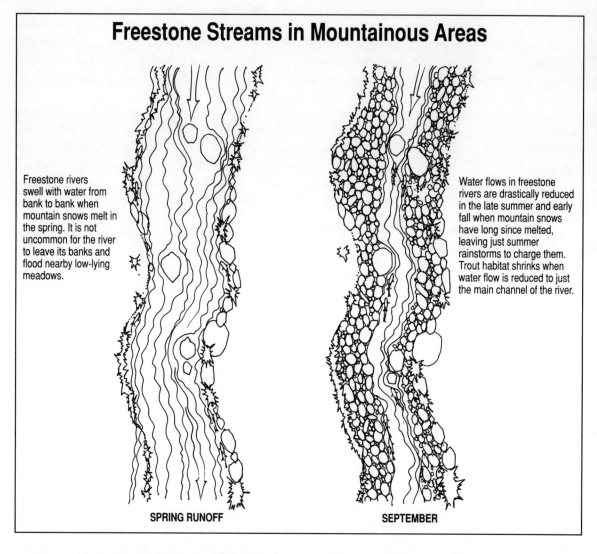

Freestone rivers swell with water from bank to bank when mountain snows melt in the spring. It is not uncommon for the river to leave its banks and flood nearby low-lying meadows.

Water flows in freestone rivers are drastically reduced in the late summer and early fall when mountain snows have long since melted, leaving just summer rainstorms to charge them. Trout habitat shrinks when water flow is reduced to just the main channel of the river.

SPRING RUNOFF

SEPTEMBER

sunlight to penetrate the water to promote plant growth anyway. The nutrient level and alkalinity of the water are also lower than most spring creeks and tailwaters.

It all comes down to a lower overall density of aquatic trout foods, but there is a lot more diversity of species among those foods. The trout can still grow to good size here, but they do it by feeding opportunistically rather than selectively. In addition, the trout miss out on a robust winter growing season when low water temperatures lower their metabolism.

You're probably wondering if there's any reason for a small-fly fisher to visit a freestone stream at all. There is. After I'd lived on the Arkansas for a while I learned that, although there may not be the numbers of small mayfly and midge species that I'd come to depend on in the South Platte tailwater, there were still populations of small flies that were important. A decent early spring blue-winged olive hatch brought many fish to the surface. It was well worth fishing, and surprisingly, the trout were selective to the size of the fly imitation fished, although it didn't matter too much what pattern I used. I also discovered that the small-fly fishing on this large freestone river occurred almost exclusively in the quiet backwaters, slicks, and gentle runs close to the banks.

The big surprise came one winter afternoon. I was looking at the river from my cabin when I saw what looked like a dimpling rise on a little slick of unfrozen water near the bank. I didn't believe it at first, but then I saw another rise and then another. I hustled down to the river and discovered that there was an isolated hatch of midges! The Dipterans weren't popping out all over the river, but there was something about this little microhabitat that was suitable for a hatch. I went back for my fly rod, and it wasn't long before I managed to land a nice brown trout on a size 20 Griffith's Gnat!

Here's the point. Although smaller aquatic insects aren't the *major* source of food for trout in a freestone river, they may still be a factor, especially in off-seasons or in microhabitats. There will be times when having a few small-fly imitations will make the difference between catching trout or not. To this day, I still have a corner of my freestone fly box reserved for size 18 through size 22 Renegades, Griffith's Gnats, Parachute Adams, and Stuck-in-the-Shuck midge patterns. They look insignificant next to the hoppers, Stimulators, streamers, Green Drakes, and big caddisflies, but they've saved the day more than once. And besides, I just like fishing small flies.

STILLWATERS

Most of the fishing I do with small flies takes place on moving water, so I'm by no means an expert about fishing them on stillwaters, but I have made a few observations regarding their use and effectiveness on lakes and reservoirs. My first observation is similar to that of small flies and freestone streams. It never hurts to have some smaller imitations on hand for those unusual sit-uations when they might be needed, although I have not frequently observed selective feeding to smaller aquatic insect species on the big water-storage reservoirs where I fish in the Rockies. As a rule, midge species are larger in the reservoirs than in moving waters. Other dominant insect species such as damselflies, dragonflies, and mayflies (most commonly *Callibaetis* spp.) all are too large to be considered small flies. The one exception I have witnessed is the occasional presence of smaller microscud species in reservoirs. It should also be noted that smaller spring-fed reservoirs may produce significant small-fly hatches and in some cases the trout feed on them as selectively as they do in a spring creek.

I have witnessed significant hatches of small mayflies and midges in beaver ponds. Although beaver pond trout tend to be opportunistic feeders, once in a while a small parachute dry-fly imitation will account for a more successful day. Small flies *have* made the difference between success and failure for me on a number of alpine lakes near where I live in Colorado. I've found trout in those high lakes to be particularly selective to small terrestrial and midge patterns. On one memorable day in Rocky Mountain National Park, I encountered a full-blown midge hatch that required size 22 emerger imitations. The trout were selective to both size and color. Tiny ant patterns have also proven important on many of the high lakes. Other than that, I usually carry some smaller Parachute Adams and a few general purpose size 18 to 22 palmer-hackled dry flies in various colors to get me by any additional small-fly problems on the high lakes.

There is no question that tailwaters and spring creeks are the Holy Grail of fishing with small flies. The trout that fin these waters are highly selective to tiny naturals. Catching them requires the highest level of fly-fishing expertise. I haunt those places and they haunt me.

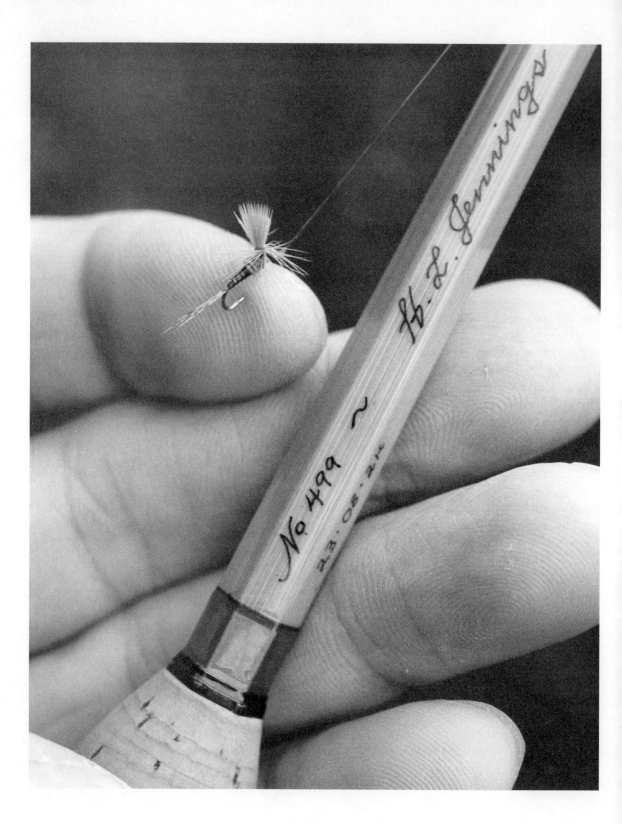

CHAPTER TWO

Tackle for Fishing Small Flies

I'm laying on the bank of Colorado's Frying Pan River, and the pale morning duns are due any minute. I can say that because they are among the most reliable mayfly hatches in the West. And like clockwork, it isn't long before the first of the duns appears on the surface. It's a good sign when a trout takes one. I wait for a few more to sputter downstream and also be eaten before I get up and quietly wade out into the river. The duns are snaking down a tongue of slick water that's in front of a large rock. Submerged boulders between the slick and me create a complex of difficult-to-read currents that are sure to produce drag. My plan is to get as close to the now regularly rising trout as I can and figure out some kind of slack-line cast to counter the drag.

I make my first cast from a position across and downstream from the trout, and it's not good. Although I've managed to pile a little bit of slack tippet on the surface, the current catches my fly almost immediately and drags it across the water. It happens so quickly that I don't even think there's time to disturb the trout. They continue to feed. The next cast doesn't fare much better, and I decide to move upstream to a straight-across casting position. My reasoning is that I'll be able to hold most of the fly line off the water with the rod and maybe buy a few more seconds of drag-free drift.

Several trout are now feeding regularly on an increasing supply of the duns. I make a test cast out of the trout's view to see what the drift looks like. My next cast is on the mark and doesn't drag, but it doesn't seduce any trout into striking. I put the following one right down the pipe and a nice rainbow nonchalantly rises and takes the fly.

It's like that for the next twenty minutes. I catch a fish here and a fish there. But then the hatch kicks up a few more notches. It seems like there's twice as many trout rising and three times as many duns on the water. All I can see are mayflies and rises. I reach that state of impenetrable concentration that sometimes happens when everything is right during a hatch. It's the reason fly fishers *don't* have to meditate. My sense of time disappears. All I see are the rises, and then my fly is there floating down toward a fish. The drift is right on the money. I even forget that I'm holding a fly rod in my hand—it becomes a natural extension of my arm. Everything is perfectly synced. I cast, I strike, I land fish, I release fish, I cast again. . . .

Eventually, the hatch goes off. I shake off the effects of the intense concentration. It doesn't always work out this way, but I look forward to the days when it does. It's as good as it gets.

I don't think you get into the zone like that by mistake. Like any other sport, fly fishing requires study, practice, and more than anything else, time on the water. There are stages of development. I believe that fishing small flies to selective trout fine-tunes an angler's awareness to the highest level. This transformation occurs not by how much equipment you bring to the encounter, but by how much you leave behind. I believe that at its best, fishing small flies puts as little as possible between me and the trout.

Part of the equation for putting as little as possible between you and the fish is your tackle. After that day on the Frying Pan, I wondered if my experience would have been different if I'd been casting an unfamiliar fly rod or if my leader design had not been one that I was used to and confident with. What if I'd been using a different design of fly line?

The details *are* important. It doesn't mean that you will ever find the perfect fly rod or the perfect leader design for every small-fly fishing situation. I fish a variety of both, depending on the water, hatches, and my mood on any given day. What is important is that you find tackle that won't *detract* from the fishing. Most well-versed fly casters can make almost any modern fly-rod taper perform well by just modifying their casting style to account for differences in the rod. I fished for years with rods that I made work. Now I try to fish rods that I don't have to consciously direct. I *want* the rod to become an extension of my arm and my eyes and my mind because then I can concentrate on the fishing.

The beauty of it all is that tackle is so subjective. A rod that works for me may be poison for you. But there are plenty of tapers and actions and lengths out there to experiment with. All I can say when it comes to tackle for angling with small flies is that you need to jump in and try it out for yourself. Pay attention to the details. Don't give up until you understand everything you need to know. And then discard everything that's not absolutely necessary. Become a minimalist.

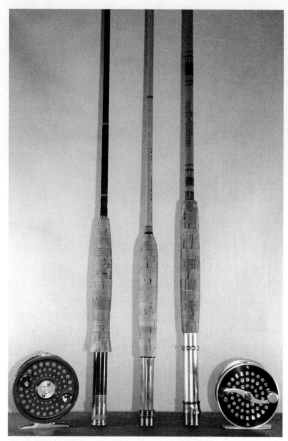

Graphite *(left)*, bamboo *(center)*, and fiberglass *(right)* fly rods all have applications for fishing small flies.

FLY RODS FOR SMALL FLIES

I've noticed that the first thing most fly fishers do when they test a rod is see how much line they can cast. Unfortunately, it's among the least important tests if you are interested in fishing small flies. Most small-fly work occurs close in. Sometimes you'll be casting little more than the leader and a few feet of fly line. Consider that when you test a rod. Cast it at the distances where you expect to be using it.

Also consider that the line weight a manufacturer recommends for a particular rod isn't gospel. If you think the rod has potential, but there's a little something missing, try it with a line weight up or a line weight down. Often a

The way that a fly rod plays a trout is an often overlooked characteristic that is important to small-fly fishermen.

rod will cast more efficiently at short small-fly fishing distances if the line weight is increased one or even two line weights above the recommended line. Don't forget to consider weight forward or long belly tapers either. Remember that fine-tuning could turn an "almost" small-fly rod into the perfect tool for you.

Always put the most emphasis on the casting qualities of the rod. I have a 7-foot, 9-inch bamboo rod that is sweet medicine when the midges are coming off the South Platte River. I almost didn't consider the rod because the common wisdom at the time was that you needed a 9-foot rod to efficiently mend the line on a stream that size. I kept trying to discount the rod, but I couldn't get out of my mind how good it felt in the hand. Finally, I took it up on the river, and it worked fine. There might have been a few spots

where a longer rod would have been more appropriate, but I was almost always able to alter my casting position to eliminate any problems. More importantly, I was fishing a rod that cast the way I liked. I didn't have to think about it at all. That meant it was just me and the trout. And that's the way I like it.

That rod had a final important attribute. I liked the way the rod played a trout. You don't hear rod makers talk much about how a rod plays a fish, but it's especially important when fishing small flies on light tippets. The only way you'll find out how a rod performs with a trout on is to go out and catch one. You may find that a rod casts very well, but when you get fish on you tend to break them off more often than you would like. If the break-offs continue on a regular basis, you may find that you're compensating for it in the way you set the hook or you develop some other quirk in your presentation. That's not good. You want everything to be seamless, fluid, light, and natural.

Bamboo

Split cane bamboo fly rods are experiencing a resurgence in popularity. Bamboo was the rod material of choice until the 1950s, when fiberglass rods took over the market. By the 1980s, graphite had taken the place of fiberglass as the rod-making material of choice. There are a lot of theories about bamboo's resurgence. Some people think that as the prices of the high-end graphite rods have approached those of a less expensive bamboo rod the leap to bamboo has become psychologically (and financially) less difficult.

Others believe that the surge of people who got involved in fly fishing in the 1980s when the movie *A River Runs Through It* came out have been around long enough that they're simply looking for something new—and bamboo is the next step. Whatever the reasons, there are a lot more bamboo rod makers out there now than there were ten years ago, and it's possible to purchase a serviceable new bamboo fly rod anywhere in cost from that of a high-quality graphite rod to the better part of a down payment on a house.

The best argument anyone can make for fishing small flies with a bamboo rod is that they just like fishing bamboo. There is no other way to justify the added cost of the rods. But there are some more down-to-earth technical considerations, too. The first argument you always hear against bamboo is that it's heavier than graphite. That's true, but to me, how the rod reacts when you try to move its mass has always been more important. There's a fluidity to casting bamboo that you don't get with many graphite rods.

Try casting a bamboo rod that loads effortlessly when you stop it at the end of the backcast and then cast a stiff graphite rod that you've really got to stick it to and see which one gives you tennis elbow first. Besides, the weight thing is a moot point for a small-fly bamboo rod. Most are 7 to 8 feet for 3- to 5-weight lines.

Here's the case for bamboo if you fish small flies. The action tends to be slower, which means you'll feel the rod load. That sensitivity may help you make more accurate casts. The slower, softer action might also help protect the light tippets required when fishing small flies. Although bamboo won't cast as far as graphite, almost all small-fly fishing takes place within 40 feet of the angler. Finally, bamboo is the only rod-making material with tapers that can be easily changed and experimented with. That means you can either find a rod that meets all your small-fly presentation needs or you can find a rod maker to build it for you.

The case against bamboo is that it *is* heavier. The slower action may not be suitable for all casting styles, especially if the caster is coming from a fast graphite background. Finally, and probably most importantly, the cost of the bamboo fly rod that you want may be prohibitive.

Nonetheless, if bamboo is suitable to any fly fishing, fishing small flies would be at the top of the list. And on the side of pure aesthetics, there are few experiences more satisfying than uncasing a fine bamboo rod, admiring and smelling the flawless varnish finish, casting it, and finally landing a trout. It is just pure sweetness.

Graphite

Graphite fly rods have come a long way *and* come back since I first started fishing them in the late 1970s. My first graphite rod had a relatively moderate action compared to some of the very fast actions now available. Surprisingly, some of the early graphite rods were actually quite soft to cast. You could feel the rod load on the backcast, and it was relatively easy to cast at short distances. Both of these characteristics are high up

Many small-fly fishermen are attracted to the qualities of the bamboo fly rod.

on my personal list of what makes a good small-fly rod. And above everything else, the graphite rods were incredibly lightweight even in 9- to 10-foot lengths. The rod diameter at the butt was about *half* of an equivalent fiberglass rod.

As rod makers gained more experience with graphite, it became the dominant rod-making material, and the rod actions became faster and faster. The faster rods were tippy, meaning that it took more energy to make them bend farther down toward the handle than a slower action rod. The big advantage of the faster rods for small-fly fishers was that they made it possible to cast a light line into moderately strong winds.

The problem was that the stiffer rods were more difficult to cast at short distances. Most small-fly fishers found that they had to change their casting style to make the rods work close-in, but those who did gained the ability to add quite long casts to their repertoire. Some fly fishers simply overlined the rods to slow them down enough to cast close in, but that cut down the distance they could achieve. In addition, some anglers felt that stiff rods in lighter line weights made it more difficult to successfully strike, play, and land fish when delicate tippets and small flies were required. The most common complaint was lack of sensitivity while playing a fish, which resulted in more break-offs.

Eventually the rod makers added rods to their inventories with tapers that slowed the rods down enough for fly fishers to achieve more comfortable casts close in. The new generation of light-line rods was more sensitive (meaning that the caster was more in touch with how the rod loaded), which resulted in more accurate casts. These rods also featured a softer tip that acted as a better shock absorber when light tippets were employed.

I saw the return to more moderate actions as a real advance for those of us who fish delicate tippets and tiny flies. And besides, it was just more fun casting a rod that you could feel load on the backcast and playing a trout on a rod that bent. Graphite has been around long enough now that there are actually a few classic graphite small-fly rods. Several of Winston's designs that used IM6 graphite such as the 8½-foot rod for a 4-weight come to mind. The Sage Light Line (LL) Series was great, too. I still fish my 9-foot LL for a 4-weight. Scott rods in the G-series and the Orvis Superfines also have a special place in many small-fly fishers' hearts.

My criterion for a small-fly graphite rod depends to some degree on where I'm fishing it. The tried-and-true rod length rules apply. For small, brushy streams, a shorter rod is in order. Bigger open water requires a longer rod. My experience in the West where I live is that an 8- to 10-foot rod with a moderate to moderately fast action for a 3- to 5-weight line is most practical. A 9-footer for a 4-weight line is a good overall compromise if you want to keep it down to one rod. Although 1- and 2-weight rods have become popular, I believe that for the average fly fisher they are most effectively used on smaller waters where wind won't be a factor. In addition, an ultralight-line rod in less than skilled hands often means that a trophy tailwater or spring creek trout caught on a small fly will end up getting played much longer than necessary before it can be released.

Neale Streeks, the respected Missouri River guide, writer, and photographer, introduced a revolutionary idea for small-fly rods and casting technique in his book, *Small Fly Adventures in the West: A Guide to Angling for Larger Trout*. Streeks makes a case for high-speed casting where a very stiff graphite rod is force-loaded for short- to medium-range casts. Force loading is achieved by pushing out a cast with "great, but smooth speed" rather than waiting for the line-assisted loading (i.e., bend) of the rod on a traditional backcast. In a speed cast the fly line doesn't load the rod, but rather it follows the rod tip that has already been force-loaded.

Since a traditional backcast with its customary stop and pause at the end to load the rod is no longer needed when speed-casting, Streeks recommends describing an oval turnover path for the fly line. It should be lower going back and higher coming forward. Basically, the faster the rod is moved the more it loads, and the more it loads the faster the resulting line speed.

The argument for the high-speed cast is that at short to moderate casting distances it allows you to make more casts per hour. More casts per hour over trout that are steadily rising to small flies often result in more hookups on tricky waters like the Missouri River where Streeks guides. The reasoning is profoundly simple—the high-speed cast means your fly is on the water more and in the air less. He believes that the high-speed cast can result in twice as many hookups over the course of a day's fishing.

High-speed casting requires a more rigid graphite rod that goes against the conventional thinking about what a small-fly rod should be. I've fooled around with the technique on waters where there are lots of steadily rising trout that keep rising for the better part of the day, and I can see the logic. Needless to say, if you adopt the technique you'll have to rethink how you strike and play trout to avoid break-offs. If you want to give it a try, but don't want to purchase a super-fast graphite rod, try underlining a softer action graphite rod by 2 to 4 line weights to speed it up.

Fiberglass

Once in a while I pull out my old 8-foot Cortland fiberglass fly rod and take it up for a day of fishing small flies on the South Platte River. It always amazes me how good that rod is. It has silky smooth casting characteristics that are between those of bamboo and graphite. Even with the lightest tippet, I seldom break trout off when playing them. The rod doesn't perform as well as a graphite rod at longer distances or in the wind,

but it's a sweetheart for slack-line casts and throwing curves. Simply put, it's a pretty good small-fly rod.

Recently, interest in fiberglass rods has been rekindled. Several rod companies are now producing them in limited numbers. If you prowl the Internet or tackle catalogs you can also find vintage fiberglass at somewhat higher prices than when they were literally a steal five or ten years ago, but most are still a bargain compared with graphite or bamboo. It's worth experimenting with them. You could very well find yourself a convert when it comes to fishing small flies. What you'll have to get used to is the considerably larger diameter of the rod in the butt section. Odds are you'll want a length in the $7\frac{1}{2}$- to 8-foot range. Anything longer tends to be a little cumbersome.

REELS

The only thing that is mandatory in a small-fly fishing reel is that the fly line pulls smoothly off of it. In most cases that boils down to the smoothest drag you can find (or afford) set as low as you can and still prevent backspooling. A reel meeting these requirements will most likely have a disk drag, but I have used very smooth ratchet-and-pawl designs. Although it's not mandatory, I like to have an exposed rim on the spool just in case I feel a need to add a smidgen more pressure to a fish by palming it. It's important to note, however, that an exposed rim is probably more valuable when playing fish on stronger terminal tackle than small-fly fishers commonly employ. Anything other than very delicate palming can snap a light tippet in a heartbeat.

What you don't want in a small-fly reel is a catchy, jumpy on-again, off-again drag. There are some pretty indelicate ratchet-and-pawl reels out there that will literally snap a light tippet when the pawl moves to the next tooth on the gear. Also, it's not necessarily the holding strength of the drag that's important. You're not going to be

Some small-fly fishers prefer an exposed rim reel *(left)*. Others like a more classic style reel *(right)*. Whatever the style, the reel should have a smooth drag.

using it to tire or turn a trout caught on a small fly tied to a fine tippet. You want a drag that will prevent backspooling and smoothly feed out the fly line.

Always remember, too, that how you reeled your line back on to the spool after the last fish you played or after that especially long cast you made will have an impact on how it feeds when a trout is hooked. You can have the best drag in the world, but if you didn't rewind your line evenly on to the spool and it knots up or feeds out erratically, you'll still break off the fish.

FLY LINES

Floating fly lines are almost always used when fishing small flies. Once in a while you'll come across a very limited local technique on larger western rivers where a sink-tip line comes into play, but it's uncommon. There are small-fly applications for full-sinking and sink-tip lines on lakes and reservoirs, too, but most often the sinking lines are used with larger fly patterns that make detecting strikes easier.

The most common debate among small-fly fishermen is whether to choose a double-taper or weight-forward fly line. It wasn't much of an argument twenty-five years ago when the double-taper line clearly aided the delicate presentations required to catch trout on small flies. At that time, the double-taper lines in the 3 to 5 weights had a longer, finer tip section than most weight-forward lines. More recently, weight-forward line design has improved to include a long, delicately tapered tip section that rivals the finest double-taper designs. Weight-forward line refinements such as long-belly tapers or Lee Wulff's triangle taper lengthen the tip section even more while smoothing the thicker weight-forward section and concentrating the weight closer to the front of the line. In terms of advantages, a double-taper line can be turned around when the front half wears out, whereas a weight-forward line will cast better in the wind and may load a graphite rod a little better on short- to medium-range casts.

Some fly fishers worry that the color of the line might spook fish. I can't make a case for that being true or false from my fishing experience, although I've heard that line color has cult status among New Zealand fly fishers. I fish pale peach, tan, light green, and other pale colors mostly because I don't like bright line colors as a matter of aesthetics. If your leader is long enough, the fly line shouldn't get close enough to the trout to spook them anyway. The bright or fluorescent colored fly lines do have a small following among small-fly fishers because they feel that they can track the fly better or follow the drift with more accuracy. The nitty-gritty is that line color probably doesn't matter that much in the United States; just don't let them catch you with a glow-in-the-dark line in New Zealand!

I *do* make a point to use the more supple fly lines rather than the stiff, superslick lines that are designed for shooting line. I think it's easier to make slack-line casts with a supple line and that it will move and bend more with the current, creating a little less drag. The more supple lines are often the less expensive, older designs. You might also be surprised by how tight a loop you can achieve with a supple line. And that comes in handy when the wind is up.

LEADER AND TIPPET MATERIAL

Everyone who fishes small flies has gotten crazy about leaders at least once. That's the way it should be, too. The leader and the tippet are what get you close to the trout. A leader that's not doing its job will result in an inefficient transfer of energy from the fly line to the leader. It could mean that your casts will be less accurate or even account for unnecessary drag when the leader's on the water. The wrong length leader or the wrong diameter tippet on a leader that *is* doing its job may give your intentions away to the trout. If that happens, even the perfect fly that is flawlessly presented will be ignored.

Before we dive into the intricacies of leaders, I should note that almost all leader designs fall into what I call the traditional proportions. That means that the heavier butt material comprises 60 percent of the length, with the next 20 percent used to step the diameter down to the tippet, which comprises the final 20 percent of the length. If you make a simple cast with a traditionally designed leader attached to it, that leader will land straight out on the water. Altering your casting stroke allows you to impart slack or curves to the leader. The slack-line leader developed by George Harvey actually lands on the water with slack in it if you make a simple, unaltered casting stroke. A little modification of the casting stroke enhances the leader's slack-line properties even more.

The first thing most small-fly fishers think about is whether to design and tie their own knotted leaders or use store-bought knotless tapered leaders. I still go back and forth between the two on a regular basis, but that wasn't always the case. I was a dyed-in-the-wool make-your-own small-fly leader kind of fisherman for many years until I recently discovered some pretty decent knotless leaders.

It seems obvious, but the good news about knotless leaders is that they are knotless. It means that if you're fishing a spring creek or tailwater with a lot of algae, vegetation, or other gunk in the flow, you're not going to have it hanging from ten different knots after every presentation. The bad news is that under certain circumstances I like leaders to have a stiffer, heavier butt section that isn't available in most knotless leaders. I think that a stiff butt section allows me to make more accurate casts and helps the leader perform better in windy conditions.

Nonetheless, small-fly knotless leaders have improved dramatically over the last five years. Most of them are marketed as spring creek leaders and come in 10- to 14-foot lengths. You'll need to experiment with the various brands to see if any of them suit your casting style and the water you plan to fish.

If you do find a knotless leader you like, but it's not quite right, a few minor alterations to the tippet and/or step-down sections will turn it into a high performance hybrid knotted/knotless leader. I have found that sometimes all it takes to make a good small-fly leader is to lengthen the tippet. If you decide that you need to go down a tippet size on a knotless leader, remember that it's designed to include a tippet that is 20 percent of its length. If you tie another 20 percent length of the lighter tippet to it, you're going to end up with too much tippet. You'll be able to tell because the tippet will be hard to manage, resulting in pileups and tangles when it lands on the water.

You can prevent this by cutting back the existing knotless tippet by 50 percent, which will in effect make it part of the step-down section of the leader. Then tie on your new tippet section, which should be 20 percent of the leader length. Of course, you won't know exactly where to cut

the tippet unless you carry a micrometer on the river, but it doesn't have to be perfect. I usually just eyeball it, but if you're worried, you can hold the tippet material you're going to tie on up against the existing tippet and make a rough judgment of where the diameters change.

I sometimes modify the step-down section of a knotless leader. Most often I'll tie in what we called a wear section when I was guiding a lot. This is usually a longer than average section of 4X or 5X material to which I'll tie the tippet. The wear section anticipates that I'll be changing flies a lot, which means the tippet will be getting cut back again and again. The longer wear section delays the inevitable chore of having to rebuild the step-down portion of the leader and doesn't seem to adversely affect the leader's performance.

Adding a Wear Section to a Tapered Knotless Leader

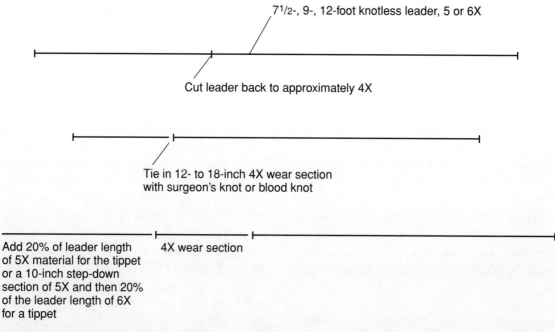

7¹/2-, 9-, 12-foot knotless leader, 5 or 6X

Cut leader back to approximately 4X

Tie in 12- to 18-inch 4X wear section
with surgeon's knot or blood knot

Add 20% of leader length
of 5X material for the tippet
or a 10-inch step-down
section of 5X and then 20%
of the leader length of 6X
for a tippet

4X wear section

As the tippet becomes shorter and shorter when flies are broken off, it can be rebuilt from the now lengthened wear section to preserve the knotless section.

Sooner or later you'll want to experiment with your own small-fly leader designs. For traditional leader designs I make the 60 percent butt section from Maxima Chameleon leader material. It's a hard, stiff nylon. Depending on the length of the leader, a typical butt section will have from three to five different diameters of material. I usually make the step-down sections and tippet from soft (limp) material, but on some designs I'll make the first couple of step-down sections from Maxima. The idea behind the limp material is that it will move, bend, and twist with the current, which will lessen drag. In addition, the soft material will stretch when a fish is on, which effectively ups its pound test rating, especially in longer lengths.

George Harvey's leader design is a radical departure from traditional leader designs. The leader, when properly adjusted by fine-tuning the length of the tippet depending on the size of the fly, will land in S-curves. When Harvey first introduced the leader more than two decades ago, he used stiff nylon for the butt section. Today, Harvey uses soft nylon for the entire leader. Harvey believes that the construction of his leader prevents drag, which allows fly fishers to use heavier tippets than those used with traditional designs. He never goes below a 5X tippet unless the hook eye of the fly he's using is too small to accommodate it. He will then go to a 6X.

I've experimented with the Harvey leader on and off over the years. It can be quite effective, especially if there isn't much wind. I've found that I need to modify my casting stroke by stopping the rod a little bit more assertively on the backcast and the forward cast to get the full benefits of the leader. Although the Harvey leader does everything he said it would, I still find myself going back to traditional design leaders mainly out of habit and because I think they perform better in windy conditions.

For a while small-fly fishers thought that braided leaders might be the answer. They provided a supersmooth transfer of energy from the fly line and added a lot of stretch to the system, which protected light tippets. The downside was that the braided section of leader tended to sink, which often pulled a tiny dry fly under with it. I don't see a lot of braided leaders on the river anymore. Another leader design incorporated a rubber band-like bungee section in the butt of the leader. The idea was that it would stretch when a large fish was on and thus protect the tippet. It sounded like a good idea, especially if, like me, you were guiding clients who weren't accustomed to protecting 6X tippets. Unfortunately, the bungees seemed prone to breakage at the knots when you could least afford it.

The key is to experiment with different leader designs until you find one that works for normal conditions where you fish. Remember that you may have to slightly modify that design once in a while to meet new conditions. No matter what leader you decide on, be sure that the butt section is the same diameter or smaller

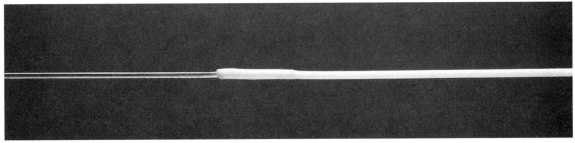

A knotless, glued connection between the leader and fly line won't hang up in the rod's line guides.

than the tip of the fly line you are attaching it to. Also, always stretch the leader out in your hands before you use it. That will straighten it.

I'm a little schizophrenic about how I tie my leaders to the fly line. For quite a while I used the Robinson/Whitlock Zap-A-Gap glue connection. You can't beat it for the smoothness of the connection, which can be crucial when landing large trout on long leaders with delicate tippets. You don't want the leader–fly line connection to snag up in the tiptop guide at a critical time. Lately, I've gone back to the reliable old nail knot with a coating of Pliobond to smooth it out so that it easily slips through the tiptop guide.

I use a blood knot to tie the heavier nylon together when I construct my own leaders and a surgeon's knot to tie the last few sections of soft material. Be sure you trim the tag sections of the knot as close as possible without nicking the knot. Stubs sticking out of knots are notorious for snagging and tangling light tippets on less-than-perfect casts or in breezy conditions. My basic working designs, which I tweak here and there, come from a George Anderson 14$^{1}/_{2}$-foot leader recipe and an A. K. Best 9$^{1}/_{2}$ leader pattern.

The length of the small-fly leader you use will depend on fishing conditions. I like a 9$^{1}/_{2}$- to 11-foot leader for standard small-fly applications. My rule of thumb is I use the shortest leader that the conditions will let me get away with. Clearly, if I'm fishing flat water with multiple trout rising or trout rising in pods, I'll opt for a longer leader. I try to draw the line at 14$^{1}/_{2}$ feet, but that's a lot of leader to control and a lot can go wrong. I'll always change my casting position first, or lengthen the tippet a bit on my 9$^{1}/_{2}$-footer if it's not too windy, before I switch over to a full-blown traditionally designed leader over 12 feet long. Windy conditions almost always require a shorter leader and/or the addition of more butt material to it.

Although you may have to modify your standard leader length to meet unusual circum-stances, it pays to stick fairly close to whatever standard length you decide on. You'll get used to that length, and it will improve your accuracy and help you get a sense of where your fly is when you can't see it.

My choice of tippet size is easy. I use the strongest (i.e., largest diameter) the trout and the size fly I'm using will let me get away with. I start with 5X if I'm fishing size 18 to size 20 flies. I'll switch to 6X if I'm having problems with microdrag. I use 6X for size 22 to size 26 flies. Once in a while conditions will require 7X, but I've found that I can cover a lot of ground with 6X if I make good slack-line casts and correctly manage my fly line. That's the way I do it, but if really light tippets are your bag, I hear you can now get nylon monofilament to 9X.

Everybody has their knot preference for tying the fly to the tippet. I don't use an improved clinch knot on small flies because I don't think it improves anything, but I do pay *very* close attention to the clinch knot when I tie it. I make sure that all the coils seat up tight against each other and that I don't nick any of them when I trim the tag end. In special situations, such as a slow eddying current during a spinner fall or when I want to impart more action to dead-drifted nymph patterns, I'll tie on the fly with a loop. I think a small fly will pivot around the loop creating a different action that may trigger a strike. I usually use a single or double surgeon's loop.

The single surgeon's loop is especially easy to tie. Simply thread the small fly on the tippet, fold the tag end back over the tippet, and then tie a single surgeon's loop. The easier-to-tie single version of the loop has held up well for me, but if you have trouble with it slipping, simply go to the standard double surgeon's loop. Some small-fly aficionados contend that a loop doubles the amount of tippet the fish sees, which doubles the chance of spooking it. All I can say is give it a try. I think the right action on the fly at the right time will override a trout's leader shyness.

Small-Fly Leaders

The majority of small-fly fishers use knotless leaders that are available in a variety of lengths, butt diameters, and tippet diameters (X). Other anglers prefer to make their own leaders by knotting sections of tippet material together to form a tapered leader. Making your own leader allows you to fine-tune the basic leader design.

Basic leader design is generally considered to be 60 percent butt section, 20 percent step-down, and 20 percent tippet. Most commonly, butt sections are made from hard nylon. Diameters range from .015 to .022 inch. As a rule of thumb, try to have the first section of butt the same diameter as the tip of the fly line.

diameter (in inches)	.022	.019	.017	.015	.013	0X .011	2X .009	4X .007	5X .006	6X .005
length (in inches)	34	25	18	15	12	10	10	10	10	30

|← ——————— hard nylon ——————— →|←——— soft nylon ———→|

This 14¹⁄₂-foot George Anderson design leader was one of the first small-fly leaders I used. I still think it's one of the best-casting, longer, small-fly leaders around. Note the somewhat large diameter butt section material that the leader begins with.

diameter (in inches)	.019	.017	.015	.013	.011	.009	.008	.007	5X .006
length (in inches)	15	14	14	14	8	7	6	5	30

|←————————— hard nylon —————————→|←—— soft nylon ——→|

A. K. Best's 9¹⁄₂- to 10-foot leader design features a very quick step-down that adds versatility for casting flies of all sizes. Note that hard nylon is used through the step-down section. This feature helps induce slack into the tippet section.
For 6X tippet, clip 5X to 5 inches and add 30 inches of 6X.
For 7X tippet, clip 6X to 5 inches and add 30 inches of 7X.

diameter (in inches)	.015	.013	.011	.009	3X .008	4X .007	5X .006
length (in inches)	19	19	19	19	15	15	36

|←————————————— soft nylon —————————————→|

George Harvey's slack-line leaders are the most radical departure from basic leader design. The leader, when properly adjusted by fine-tuning the length of the tippet, will land in S curves. The first incarnation of Harvey's leader used stiff nylon for the butt section. Today Harvey uses soft nylon for the entire leader.
For a 6X tippet, cut the 5X back to 15 inches and add a 36-inch 6X tippet. Adjust the length of the tippet to the fly you're casting to get the desired slack-line presentation.

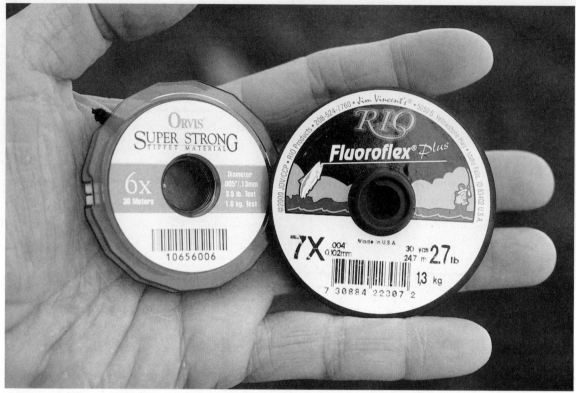

Regular nylon leader material *(left)* and fluorocarbon leader material have special applications when fishing small flies.

Fluorocarbon leader material has become quite popular in recent years. The party line is that its lower light refractivity index should make it more difficult for the trout to see than nylon. The fluorocarbon is also more abrasion-resistant than monofilament. The downside is that it costs a lot more than monofilament. There is also some concern that it doesn't deteriorate as quickly in the environment as nylon does, but this may not be as bad as it sounds for fly fishers who only use short lengths of the material.

I was initially drawn to fluorocarbon because I thought it could give me an edge, and that's what fishing small flies is all about. I've found that fluorocarbon does indeed give me a clear advantage for many stillwater fishing applications. On moving water I've found that sometimes it helps when dead-drifting small nymph patterns, but at other times it doesn't. It seems like the slower the water is moving the better it works. I do think that the fluorocarbon allows me to go up one X value in tippet size when fishing below the surface because of its lower light refractivity index, but the material is stiffer than nylon, which may inhibit the fly's action.

Surprisingly, fluorocarbon seems to have less impact when I fish dry flies. It occasionally seems to make a difference on top, but it hasn't been the across-the-board higher success rate that I thought it would give me. Most likely it works better under some light conditions but not others. It *is* more difficult to see on the water's surface because it tends to sink. I've found myself having to grease it three or four feet behind the fly so that I could see the general area where the

Small flies tend to clump up and are difficult to see in a compartment-style fly box. They can also be blown away by the wind.

fly was! I had not realized how much I relied on the floating nylon leader to track the whereabouts of a small fly that was not visible on the surface. Once again, I found that the fluorocarbon material is less flexible than soft nylon monofilament, which may create microdrag.

I've come to the conclusion that under most conditions, I only need a fluorocarbon tippet for river and stream fishing, but for lakes, an entire fluorocarbon leader or at least a half-leader length of fluorocarbon makes a difference. If I'm tying fluorocarbon to fluorocarbon I use the same knots I use for nylon, but I pay special attention to clinch knots on small hooks that may pull out if they aren't cinched up very tight. I also use the same knots when I'm tying fluorocarbon to nylon but I pay even more attention. I have had surgeon knot and even blood knot fail-

ures, but I've found that if I make sure the knots are cinched up tight they will hold.

OTHER STUFF
Fly Boxes

Compartment-style fly boxes don't cut it when you fish small flies. It's just too easy to load too many flies into one compartment. They end up clumped into a furry ball. Also, if you're facing the wrong way on a windy day and you open your compartment fly box, you can expect most of your small flies to blow away. About the only advantage to a compartment box at all is that you can carry about a million flies—if you call that an advantage.

Get ripple or flat foam insert boxes and arrange your fly patterns so you can see what you have. Since they are securely imbedded in

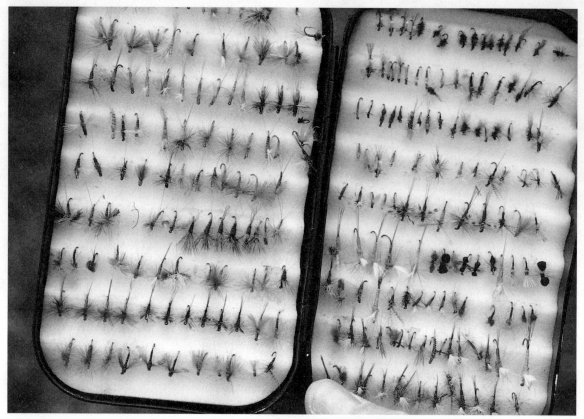

A ripple-foam fly box displays small flies so that they can be seen and prevents the wind from blowing them away.

the foam, you can open the box even when the wind is blowing. The flies can be arranged in a variety of ways. I like to have nymph and deep-emerger patterns in one box and dry flies and near-surface emergers in another one. I find it helpful to organize midge imitations by color and mayflies by species. The microcaddisfly, terrestrials, and experimental imitations all have separate sections in the box.

I guided for a long time so it's only natural that I got into a little guide-itis on the fly boxes. I had a million of them and a million flies. When you guide on a river where small flies are important, it's easy to think that you may go through a dozen or two flies of a single size of an imitation. Depending on a client's skill level it doesn't take much to break off a small-fly, especially if he isn't

used to playing a trout on a light tippet. Over the years you also find patterns that can save the day, so you stock up on them. Of course, you can't forget three or four dozen apiece of the old standbys in a variety of hook sizes. And it goes on and on until your vest is so full you look like the Michelin man.

You don't need all that when you're fishing small flies for yourself. Keep it to two boxes—dry flies and subsurface flies. It's all you'll need. They *are* small flies. You'll be able to get a bunch of them in the box. You'll be happier. If you feel that having only two fly boxes strips you of all your power, leave the other twenty or thirty of them in the car for security. You can walk out and get them if you need them. You'll be surprised at how few trips you make back to the car.

Paste and gel fly floatants along with a desiccant-type drying powder are important when fishing tiny dry flies.

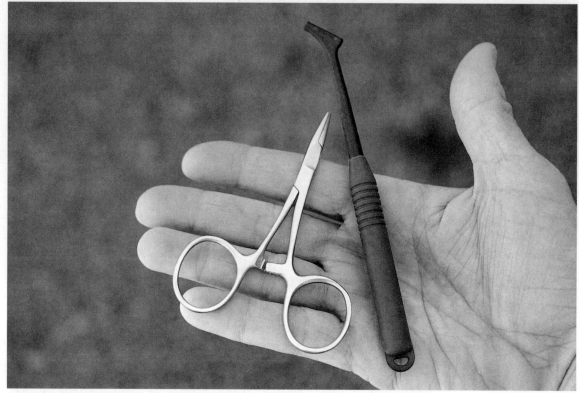

A hemostat-style pliers *(left)* or a Ketchum release tool is useful for taking tiny hooks out of trout.

Fly Floatant

I always carry a paste and gel fly floatant and a container of the desiccant-type fly-drying powder. The paste floatant comes in handy for greasing leader sections when I want them to float or when I want to add floatant to just the suspender portion of a tiny suspender fly. The gel-type floatant is good for treating hackle. The desiccant powder is indispensable for drying out tiny CDC and other floating flies. Sometimes treating a fly in the powder will lighten its color just enough to make it visible on the water's surface. That visibility can be the difference between success and failure.

Release Tool

I carry a Ketchum release tool when I fish my home waters and more and more it's all I carry when I'm visiting other waters. I use the model designed for small flies. It's the size of a pencil and allows me to release a trout without ever taking it out of the water.

If you decide to use a release tool, be advised that it will take a little practice to get used to it. You may also end up having to play the fish a bit longer than you would if you used a landing net. The tool works much better on small flies that have been debarbed.

Some small-fly fishers use their regular hemostat-style pliers in the same way I use the release tool. It's never worked well for me, but it's worth a try. Whether you use the pliers to release fish or not, you'll probably want a pair to hold flies when tying them to the tippet, for pulling out flies that get caught in your shirt, net, skin, or waders, and for taking flies out of the fish if you use a net.

If you prefer a landing net or need it to assist in taking photo, use one made of a soft material and try to get the fish back into the water as quickly as possible.

Polarized Sunglasses, Magnifiers, and Light
The best small-fly angling occurs when you can stalk and hunt fish. You'll need polarized sunglasses to do this. Never leave home without them. I like brown tints for places where better contrast is important and gray tints for where I need accurate color recognition.

If your eyes are older, you're going to need some kind of magnification to select and tie tiny flies to your leader. It's your choice—flip downs, readers, high-power bifocals in your prescription glasses—whatever it takes. It doesn't hurt to put an extra pair in the back of your vest either.

When light conditions are less than perfect, a miniature light source will help you see a tiny fly and illuminate your attempt to tie it to the tippet. It will also allow you to stay on the water in the twilight when the blue-winged olive or pale morning dun spinner fall occurs. You don't want to be standing there with the perfect fly and no way to see to tie it on.

I won't go into the particulars of waders, vests (or no vest), clothing, and other gear because so much of it comes down to each angler's specific needs and tastes. What I will say is that there are two ways to go as a small-fly fisher. You can buy all the doo-dads, gadgets, and junk in the world, but in the end it may only weigh down your vest. Be judicious. There are a lot of things to consider, such as leader design, fly boxes, rod and reel, and fly line, but once you've made up your mind, leave it at that. Carry only the bare essentials. Be light. Have as little as possible between you and the trout.

CHAPTER THREE

The Power of Observation

It's the height of the guide season on the South Platte and I'm doing what I always do—watching trout *and* trout fishermen. I like to get my guests on the river early in the day before the wind comes up, dial them into the style of fishing that's going to be most productive, and then let them fish. Every guide has their own style. It seems like the most popular style nowadays is for the guide to hang on their client's elbows telling them where to put every cast, when to strike, and even when to have lunch.

I'm old-fashioned. I try to take the time to get the client pointed in the right direction, iron out a few kinks, and then let them work out the details on their own. If I see problems, I can step up and put my two cents in. My fishermen may catch a trout or two less than the guy with the guide attached to his elbow, but the trout they do catch will be their own. I figure if a guide tells you where to cast, when to strike, how to play the fish, and when to land it, it's the guide's trout. If I was being guided, I'd rather not catch a fish under those circumstances.

Anyway, once my clients get started, I mosey upstream to look for the trout that we'll fish to next. There is a subtle drift line tucked close into a grassy bank that I always watch. Today a few trout are quietly tipping up to the leftovers from an early-morning Trico spinner fall. The rises are soft and mysterious—like a stranger blowing a kiss from across the street.

I'm watching the fish when two fly fishers approach the river. They're busy jabbering about something and just walk right up to the edge of the water and unhook their flies from the hook-keepers on their rods. Without a moment's hesitation they splash into the river and begin dead-drift nymphing in the main channel. The trout on the opposite bank actually keep rising the whole time they're fishing and they never see them. It doesn't take long before the two fishermen decide the action might be better somewhere else and wander downstream.

Those trout could have been their trout. If they would have taken just a second to look at the river, they probably would have seen them. And I bet those are a couple of big trout. I know a way that you can wade across the river and get into position for a good presentation to them, too.

I glance back downstream at my clients, who I have never let out of my sight, and I can see they're getting antsy. Although I know there are plenty of trout where they're fishing, I can tell they're ready to move on. I walk downstream to meet them. On our way back upstream I stop across from the rising trout and quietly stand. A little dimple smudges the water's surface. Another little dimple shows four feet upstream from it. Nobody says anything.

"There's a spot just up here a ways," I say. I know I'm being naughty, but I'm keeping those risers for myself. My guys had their chance. We were looking right at them.

Every small-fly fisherman knows that the rings left on the water's surface by a rising trout are an important event. They also realize that there is more to seeing trout than just watching those rings, whether they are obvious or not. You need to be able to spot trout feeding on and near the water's surface *and* the more difficult-to-see feeding activity under the surface.

The way to see more trout is to systematize your observations. The first step is to simply take a few minutes before you begin fishing to con-sciously observe the water. There's an easy way to remind yourself to take this step. Just don't tie a fly to the tippet until you've taken a considered look at the water. A good place to observe the river is from higher ground that overlooks it. If you're far enough away from the water you won't have to worry about spooking the trout. In situa-tions where you think the trout might be able to spot you, it's wise to slowly move down the hill a ways so that it breaks up your silhouette.

When there are no handy overlooks, make a quiet approach to the river. Use streamside vege-tation to break up your silhouette wherever pos-sible. A particularly open meadow section of a

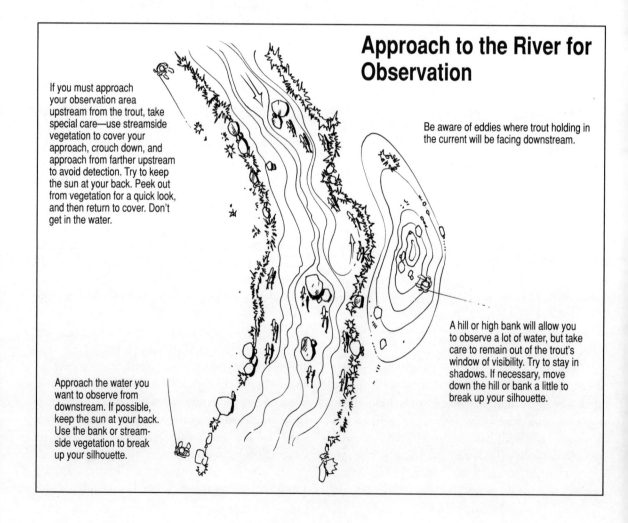

Approach to the River for Observation

If you must approach your observation area upstream from the trout, take special care—use streamside vegetation to cover your approach, crouch down, and approach from farther upstream to avoid detection. Try to keep the sun at your back. Peek out from vegetation for a quick look, and then return to cover. Don't get in the water.

Be aware of eddies where trout holding in the current will be facing downstream.

A hill or high bank will allow you to observe a lot of water, but take care to remain out of the trout's window of visibility. Try to stay in shadows. If necessary, move down the hill or bank a little to break up your silhouette.

Approach the water you want to observe from downstream. If possible, keep the sun at your back. Use the bank or stream-side vegetation to break up your silhouette.

spring creek or tailwater may require you to crouch down or stand a little farther back from the bank. Plan your approach to bring you to the river downstream from the area you want to observe with the light at your back, if possible. Once you're in position, take a few minutes to give the water an overall scan. Most anglers do a version of this without even thinking about it when they walk up to the river. Do the same thing, except make a point to think about what you see. You'll be surprised.

SURFACE AND NEAR-SURFACE SMALL-FLY FEEDING ACTIVITY INDICATORS

You'll immediately spot most rising trout, but look for the less obvious ones. Take the time to carefully inspect any water that's in the shadows for dimpling trout. Pay special attention to the banks where a trout may be quietly rising just inches from the shore. Look at the shallow water where you wouldn't expect a riser to be. Check out the air over the river and its surface for any insects that may be hatching. Visible insects on the water greatly increase the chances of surface-feeding activity.

If you see insect activity try to collect a sample and determine if they are midges, mayflies, microcaddisflies, tiny stoneflies, or terrestrials. Once you know what they are, figure out what they're doing. Are they hatching, laying eggs, simply hovering over the water, diving back in the water to lay eggs, being blown to the surface, or did you just disturb them when you kicked up the streamside vegetation as you approached the river? If there's more than one species of insect, make a note of it. Remember the size, color, and shape (silhouette) of the insects you've observed. If there is concentrated insect activity, but you don't see any trout rising, bide your time. There is a good chance they will.

The shape of the disturbance that a rising trout makes on the water's surface, called the *rise-form,* will give you a wealth of information about what fly pattern to use and how to fish that pattern. It's crucial to determine whether the trout are taking insects from the surface or from just below the surface when you see a riseform. The most reliable way to do this is to pick a single hatching adult on the water's surface and watch it as it drifts downstream. It's a good indication that *some* adults are being eaten if a trout takes it. The next determination to make is whether the trout are feeding predominantly on top. Do this by watching the adult insects float downstream as a whole. If you see trout picking them off regularly you can be reasonably sure that the majority of trout are on top.

Pay particular attention to the riseform if you see surface disturbances, but only the occasional adult insect is being eaten. Further observation will probably reveal that the surface disturbance has a moundlike shape, but the trout's head is not visible near the surface, or that the trout are porpoising with only the dorsal fin and tail visible. Maybe all you see is a swirl and then a trout's tail, or in shallow water just the tail poking up out of the water. These are all indications that the trout are feeding just below the surface on emerging nymphs or pupae, except the one where the trout's tail is visible in shallow water. That trout is feeding on emergers the moment they leave the streambed.

An often taught fly-fishing class example of how to determine if the trout are feeding on adults or emergers is to carefully observe the riseform. A bubble in the middle of it indicates that the trout has taken an adult because its mouth broke the water's surface and in the process pushed a little air through its gill plates, forming the bubble. That's often the way it plays out, too. But a satisfied wiggle of the tail after a trout takes an emerger will also form a bubble. Or a quick turn after taking an emerger might swirl the surface enough for a bubble to form. The point is that the only way to be certain is to make careful observations every time you see rising fish. I still get fooled once in a while to this day.

Riseforms

Fly fishermen throughout history have placed great emphasis on riseforms and recorded a large catalog of riseform types. The late Pennsylvania spring creek and small-fly specialist Vince Marinaro studied the riseform in depth in his books *A Modern Dry Fly Code* (1950) and *In the Ring of the Rise* (1976), as did the British spring creek anglers John Goddard and Brian Clarke in *The Trout and the Fly* (1980).

Marinaro made important observations of the basic mechanics of trout rising to take insects from the surface of the slow-moving water that typifies many spring creeks and tailwaters. His observations led him to conclude that trout rise to an insect or an artificial fly in three ways: the simple rise, the compound rise, and the complex rise. All three rises begin with the trout in a holding position where it can observe what is floating downstream on the surface and near the surface. The type of rise the trout makes depends on the confidence it has in the food source.

The **simple rise** usually takes place during a major hatch where the trout are confident about the food source. When a trout spots the insect it goes upward toward it while at the same time drifting downstream with the current. When the trout and the fly meet at the surface, it will either take the fly right away or refuse it.

The **compound** rise is essentially a longer simple rise where the trout takes more time to examine the food source (or artificial fly) as it drifts along with it downstream. The compound rise is almost always an indication that the fish has less confidence in the food source. It will continue to drift downstream with the insect, constantly inspecting it, until it either takes it or refuses it.

The **complex rise** occurs when the trout has considerable doubt about the food source (or

Simple Rise

The simple rise is most often encountered when trout are feeding confidently during a major hatch. When the trout spots the insect, it moves up toward it while at the same time drifting downstream with the current. When the trout and the fly meet at the surface, the trout will either take the fly or refuse it.

Compound Rise

The compound rise is essentially a simple rise wherein the trout takes more time to examine the food source. It will continue to drift downstream with the fly and may even turn a little before it either takes or refuses it.

Complex Rise

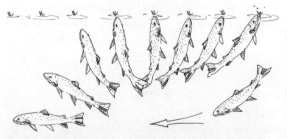

The complex rise occurs when the trout has considerable doubt about the food source. As the trout drifts downstream with the fly, it will stay farther away from it and take longer to inspect it. When the fly begins to get downstream of the trout, it will either turn and quickly pursue the fly or refuse it. Vince Marinaro says that once the trout decides to turn downstream and chase the fly, he will never refuse it.

artificial fly). As the trout drifts downstream with the insect, it will stay a little farther away from the fly, delaying active inspection. The rise will end here if the trout sees something it doesn't like. If the trout still isn't quite sure it will continue drifting downstream with the fly until it begins to get downstream from him. At this time the trout will either refuse the fly or turn facing downstream and quickly pursue it. Marinaro contends that once the trout has made the decision to turn downstream and chase the fly it will *never* refuse it.

The way the trout rises to the fly is important from a tactical point of view. Although a drag-free drift is important for almost all presentations, it's especially crucial during a compound or complex rise when the trout carefully inspects the fly. Any drag at this critical time means curtains to a fly fisher's aspirations. Over the years I have observed these rises in a variety of situations and during a variety of different hatches. My experience has been that it's a lot more likely that you'll run into both compound and complex rises when smaller insects are hatching.

Marinaro's discoveries were concerned with how the trout rises to the fly from its holding or observation position. The rises give clues to how well the trout are accepting your imitations. A simple rise means confidence. A compound rise indicates less confidence, and a complex rise means you could be skating on thin ice. My policy is to switch flies after a couple of refusal rises if I'm confident that my drifts are drag-free. If the refusals are coming out of a compound or a complex rise, it is sometimes effective to use the same fly in a size or two smaller.

The actual disturbance that the rise causes on the surface is the riseform. It's another rich source of information for small-fly fishers. Careful observation of a riseform will tell you whether the trout is feeding on the surface or just below it, what life stage of the insect the trout is feeding on, and whether that insect is ac-

tive or not. And besides, a rising trout is nothing short of poetry. If I was told I could never fly-fish again, I would still go to the river just to see trout rise.

Fly fishers have been avid catalogers of trout riseforms for hundreds of years. I've read accounts that reference as many as fifty different riseform types or as few as fifteen. The language describing the riseforms is often not consistent, which means the same riseform may be known by different names depending on when you lived or where you live now. Not all of the described riseforms are important to small-fly fishermen either. Trout are most often found rising to small insects in slow- to moderate-moving water. This is related to where the immature forms of the insects live and then hatch, but more importantly it's just hard for the trout to see and catch small insects in faster water. The energetics of feeding on small insects in slow-moving water makes more sense, too. Although the trout has to make more rises than it would chasing down larger insects in faster water, the small insects are often very plentiful in the slow-moving water. He'll consume far more calories than he uses up if all he has to do is sip the tiny insects from the surface of the slowly moving water.

The following riseforms are most often encountered by small-fly fishermen. Remember, too, that unless these riseforms occur on absolutely still water, the disturbance that you see on the water's surface will always be downstream from where the trout took the insect. Try to observe the riseform at the moment when a trout takes the insect. A riseform deforms quickly after the take and much of the information that it holds is lost.

Bulges. Bulges are one of the riseforms that can fool you. At first you may think it indicates surface feeding simply because the surface is disturbed, but closer examination reveals that a bulge looks like a mound of water. It's typically the result of a trout taking small, emerging

Bulge

Sip

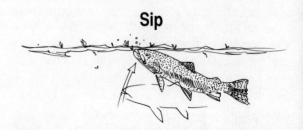

insects just below the surface. The diagnostic feature of the bulge is that you won't see any part of the trout—just the bulging mound of water and perhaps a swirl at the end if the trout turns. If you observe trout that are steadily bulging in slower water, it is an almost certain sign that a hatch of small mayflies or midges is imminent. The onset of bulging behavior often takes place at the beginning of the hatch. Bulging is a common sight on spring creeks and tailwaters where trout feed on large populations of small aquatic insects. It's less frequently observed on freestone rivers, although I have seen it in quiet backwaters where trout are rising to winter hatches of midges.

Boils. A boil is a more energetic bulge. The trout is still feeding below the surface, but there is a greater surface disturbance. Sometimes there is even a little splash. Boils are not as important to small-fly fishers because they usually indicate that the trout are taking larger emerging insects. You will occasionally see boils to some species of smaller caddisflies during emergence. Once in a while the trout will boil when taking small mayflies, too. This is particularly true with pale morning duns and their relatives.

Sips. A sipping rise is the bread-and-butter of small-fly angling. It occurs when the trout are taking small mayfly duns, midge pupae hanging in the meniscus, midge adults, terrestrials, and mayfly spinners. Sips occur in slower-moving water. You may observe just the tip of the trout's nose during the take on a sipping rise. If there are duns on the surface, you'll see them disappear. If you don't see adult insects being taken, there is a good chance that midge pupae trapped

in the meniscus are being eaten. More than one fly fisher has been fooled into thinking that a barely perceptible sipping rise is the work of a small trout or chub. My experience is that the more subtle the sip the *larger* the trout.

I pay special attention to single sippers. Fly fishers typically notice sippers lined up in the slow-moving current of a flat or a pool where a steady stream of food is supplied. There are often dozens of rising trout. The single sipper is always off by itself. I look for them tucked up tight against a bank or against a rock. When they rise, the surface disturbance doesn't result in the classic perfect ring of expanding ripples, but rather in what my friend John Gierach calls a "half moon" rise. It's a rise that's so close to the bank or a rock that it's only half a ring of ripples. The feeding behavior of the single sipper is typically erratic, which is why they so often go unnoticed. But these may be the largest trout of all. The single sippers are trout that are keyed into the subtle microcurrents that carry food close to the banks where they can maintain their hiding cover and eat at the same time. It's prime big-trout habitat.

In the fly-fishing literature, sipping riseforms may also be referred to as smutting or dimpling rises, but they all result from trout taking small emerging or adult midges, mayflies, or terrestrials in slower-moving water. No matter what you call them, the important thing to do is identify the activity as being on the surface or in the meniscus.

Head-to-Tail. I always view the head-to-tail rise, also known as the porpoising rise, with excitement and fear. It's close to a sure sign the trout are feeding on something small, usually

Head-to-Tail Rise

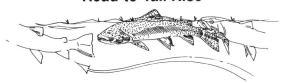

Headless Head-to-Tail Rise

Wedge Rise

Head Rise

midges, but also blue-winged olives and to a lesser degree other small mayflies. Ernest Schwiebert observed in his book, *Trout,* that head-to-tail rises often indicate trout are taking spent spinners or insects trapped in the surface film. The excitement of seeing head-to-tail rises is that I know I will have something to cast to; the fear is that head-to-tail risers are often quite selective. I've fished to porpoising trout during winter midge hatches that just drove me nuts. No matter what I threw at them and no matter how perfect my presentation was I'd be lucky to land a couple of trout after four hours of casts to steadily rising fish!

It is critically important to determine whether a head-to-tail riser is taking from just below the surface or on top. If the trout are keying on emergers near the surface, you'll see mostly the back of the fish behind the head, the dorsal fin, and the tail. The head itself will be conspicuously invisible. I call it a headless head-to-tail rise. If the trout are taking adults from the surface, you will see its head as it gracefully porpoises head-to-tail. It's not always easy to make this determination. If you're having trouble, try to watch a single dun. If you see it disappear and then observe others consistently disappearing, figure the trout are on top. Neale Streeks and Ernest Schwiebert both describe bubbles left

after porpoising rises as an indication that the trout are on top.

Trout are opportunists, so figure that at the beginning of the hatch, when there are more emergers available, the trout will feed below the surface on them. That's when you're most likely to see the headless head-to-tail rise. As the hatch progresses and more and more duns are on the surface or more and more midge pupae and adults get caught up in the meniscus, the trout will feed on top. Look for the more classic head-to-tail rise then.

Wedges. The wedge rise, which is closely related to the head-to-tail rise, is not common where I fish, but I have seen it enough during rises to midges, and less commonly to blue-winged olives, that it bears mention. The wedge is actually not a rise at all, but rather the protrusion of the trout's tail or dorsal fin as it lazily sways back and forth just under the surface while picking off nymphs or pupae. The wedge always occurs in slow-moving water when there are significant numbers of immature aquatic insects in the drift. This most often takes place when a hatch is imminent.

Head Rises. The head rise is a fairly new term that describes the riseform where a trout actually lifts its entire head out of the water while feeding. In the past, head rises were lumped into the head-to-tail riseform category.

Gulping Rise

Tailing Trout

My experience with head rises has occurred almost exclusively during heavy Trico spinner falls.

Gulping rises. The gulping rise is a head rise where the trout greedily make head rises while they gobble up heavy hatches or spinner falls. Sometimes the trout will slowly swim a little ways upstream excitedly gulping this way and that, then pause and drift back downstream to their holding position and do it all over again. A distinguishing characteristic of the gulping rise is that the trout develop a predictable feeding rhythm. As excited as the feeding is, it should be noted that both head risers and gulpers will at times be spooky, so a careful approach is required.

Head risers and gulpers often make a distinctive plopping or lip popping kind of sound as they rise. Hearing that sound on the river is as close as it gets to big-game hunting for me. It sends shivers down my spine because I know even the largest trout are up on the fin.

Tailing. Tailing trout technically aren't rising at all. They are feeding in shallow water, nose down to the bottom, with their tail sticking up out of the water's surface. I've seen this behavior on spring creeks around shallow weed beds

where the trout are kicking out microscuds and weed-loving mayfly nymphs. I've actually observed trout working in tandem where one tailing trout is rummaging around the vegetation and another is directly downstream from him gobbling up anything that ends up in the drift. Whether the upstream trout knows the freeloader is there is anybody's guess. You should also expect to find trout tailing over shallow muddy or silty bottoms where midge pupae are emerging.

SPOTTING SUBSURFACE FEEDING ACTIVITY INDICATORS

A rising trout is pretty hard to miss most of the time. Trout holding and feeding below the surface are a different story. The single most important benefit I gained from more than ten years of guiding fly fishers on Colorado's South Platte River tailwater system was that I learned to spot trout under the surface. Most fishermen aren't naturals when it comes to spotting trout. Guides develop the skills because they are on the water day in and day out constantly looking for fish. It takes practice and the intuition that results from paying attention to the minutest details.

The best place to begin improving your subsurface trout-spotting skills is the same place you started when you learned to look for surface activity. Start by selecting a good location to observe the river and approach it in a way that won't spook the trout. Clear your mind of all the stuff you usually think about at the beginning of a day's fishing. Pay attention to the river. Successful angling with small flies demands careful observation. If you don't see any rising trout, you'll have to look *into* the water.

Tools for Spotting Subsurface Trout
Polarized Sunglasses. The single most important item of equipment for spotting trout below the surface is a pair of glare-reducing polarized sunglasses. I prefer laminated glass lenses for my

polarized sunglasses, which clearly makes me old-fashioned. Most Polaroids are made of optical quality plastic nowadays. A laminated lens consists of a polarized film placed between layers of optical quality glass. The laminate is required because glass cannot be polarized. The reason I prefer the glass lenses is that they hold up. Optical quality plastic lenses cost almost the same as glass, but I've found that no matter what the manufacturer's claim, the plastic will scratch. If I'm lucky I get two years out of a pair, whereas I have one pair of glass lens Polaroids that I've used for twenty years. They are just now beginning to delaminate around the edges.

Top of the line polarized sunglasses can be pretty expensive, but less expensive plastic Polaroids have improved over the years. In the past, lower-quality plastic was used for the lenses, and you could figure they'd be scratched within a week, but there are some pretty good products out there now. Since I wear prescription glasses, I was attracted to the type of Polaroids that fit over my regular prescription glasses. These have several advantages for me because I have a bifocal prescription. The fit-over style glasses let me use my bifocals, which saves me the additional cost of prescription Polaroids with bifocals.

I also shoot photographs with a polarizing filter when I'm fishing. If I'm wearing my prescription Polaroid sunglasses, everything goes black when I adjust the filter on the camera. It means I have to dig out my regular eyeglasses and put them on and then put my prescription Polaroids back on when I'm finished. I've equipped my fit-over style Polaroids with an eyeglass holder so all I have to do when I want to take a photograph is remove the glasses and let them hang around my neck. Finally, I like to be able to take the fit-over sunglasses off to see what things look like in unpolarized light. Sometimes this has helped me identify a trout in especially difficult conditions.

The tint of the polarized lenses in your sunglasses will affect the way you see trout. An array of tints is now available, but the majority of small-fly fishermen still prefer brown or gray. The brown lens gives higher contrast, which tends to sharpen images, but because it filters out much of the blue-gray light, your perception of colors will be altered. A gray lens offers truer colors but doesn't provide as much contrast as the brown lens. My rule of thumb is brown tints work best for clear water on sunny days when I'm mainly looking for shapes. Gray tints work better in cloudy or low-light conditions when I want to pick up the color of a trout. Yellow lenses will work when maximum contrast is needed for low-light conditions, but you almost need to carry another pair of dark sunglasses just in case the sun comes out. If you want that kind of range in your sunglasses, a photochromatic polarizing lens might be better than carrying two pairs of sunglasses.

No matter what kind of polarized sunglasses you finally decide on, remember that you may have to move around on the streambank a little for them to be most effective. A minor change in position will often be enough to put the polarized lenses in the optimum position to reduce glare on the water's surface.

You're probably beginning to think that I'm a little obsessive about sunglasses. You're right. Fishing small flies at the highest and most challenging levels requires the angler to first spot and then stalk trout. There is nothing more thrilling. A decent pair of polarized sunglasses is where you start.

Head Gear. A good hat is pretty low-tech, but it will improve your ability to see into the water. I like long-bill fishing caps for several reasons. Although the narrow brimmed fedora-style canvas packer hats have become all the rage on the streams where I fish, I've stuck with an old-timey long, broad-bill cap. I think the bill shades my eyes, which helps me see into the water better. In bad light conditions, I can roll the bill down around my face with my hands to form a

Polarized sunglasses, a long-billed cap, and a compact pair of binoculars are important tools for small-fly fishers.

darkened "tunnel" that helps me see into the water. In addition, the underside of the bill on my hat is a very dark green, which absorbs the light that reflects back up from the water. A light color under the brim can actually reflect light back into your eyes, which is undesirable.

Binoculars. A final item of equipment that you may want to consider is a pair of compact binoculars or a lightweight monocular. Binoculars can be particularly useful when you are just learning to spot trout. They will help you determine if what you saw was a tailing trout or a stick poking up out of the water. The binoculars will also allow you to observe the river from a greater distance to avoid spooking trout. If you are specifically hunting for large trout, binoculars can be especially helpful. They will allow you to cover more water from one position and help

you determine more accurately the size of the fish you are observing. My binoculars are an inexpensive pair of compact 8 X 20 wide-angle glasses which take up very little room in my fly-fishing vest.

Seeing Trout Under the Surface

So now that you are equipped to see trout, the question is what do you look for? Although the easiest trout to see are those that in some way disturb the water's surface, learning to spot them may not be the most important skill for the observant small-fly angler to learn. A more fundamental and difficult skill is the ability to see trout in their feeding, holding, and hiding lies. This means spotting trout as they go about their business *beneath* the water's surface. These trout don't reveal themselves with telltale tracks left on the

Trout Over Sand

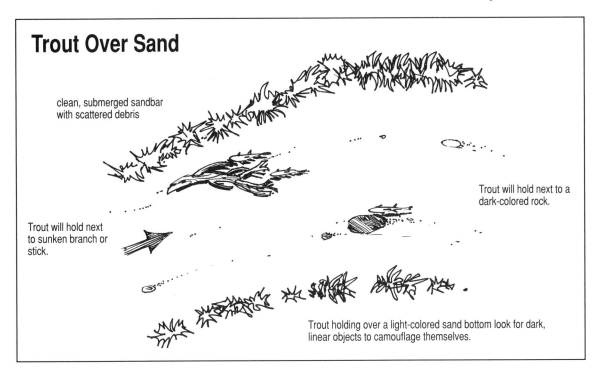

clean, submerged sandbar
with scattered debris

Trout will hold next to a
dark-colored rock.

Trout will hold next
to sunken branch or
stick.

Trout holding over a light-colored sand bottom look for dark,
linear objects to camouflage themselves.

water's surface. You'll need to look *into* the river to see them.

Start with the water that's in the shadows. It's easier to see into the river where there is no glare. Look for trout that may be feeding under the water's surface. If you find yourself in a position where the glare on the water's surface does obscure your view, you may have to quietly move a little upstream or downstream to a position where the glare is less severe.

There's an obvious reason why it's difficult to spot a trout in the river. They don't want you to see them. It's to the trout's advantage to not be visible to predators. They are particularly attuned to danger from above, such as eagles, osprey, herons, mergansers, kingfishers, and fly fishers. When you're trying to see a trout under the water's surface, you're working against millions of years of evolution geared toward preventing you from seeing them. It's why trout are colored the way they are, why they hang out in the parts of

the river they do, and why they behave as they do.

Have you ever considered why most trouts' bellies are white? I think it might have evolved to help diffuse the shadow that they cast on the streambed. Under the right conditions, the light-colored belly helps reflect light back down to the streambed, which tends to tone down the shadow. It means you may have to look just a little closer to see a trout's shadow. You may also have noticed how the light colors on the trout's belly progressively get darker as they move up the trout's side. The dorsal sides of most trout species are quite dark. That makes a trout hard to spot when it's over a dark mottled bottom. If the bottom is light colored, a motionless trout may appear like a rock or a sunken branch.

None of this means that a trout holding over a sandbar is invisible. When they do they're pretty obvious, but just try catching them. It's incredibly difficult. Maybe the trout have developed some behavioral habits that compel them to be especially alert when in a vulnerable position.

Movement is the most obvious clue to a trout's presence. Flashing happens when the fish is suspended in the water busily eating emergers. After the trout devours an insect, it quickly turns to get back into its feeding lie—that's when you see the flash of its belly or flank.

Flashing is the most obvious movement you will observe. More often the indications are subtle. You might spot the movement of a gill plate, or see the trout open its mouth to take an emerging nymph. Perhaps you'll notice the flicker of the trout's tail as it realigns itself in the current. Sometimes you'll spot a trout's movements when what looks like a rock shifts upstream just a little bit, or when what you thought was a rock's shadow moves.

You'll see more trout if you avert your vision slightly, a trick I learned when I was a kid. I was interested in astronomy, and I found that the most acute vision is actually several degrees to one side of straight ahead. When I looked up at the night sky, I'd notice that I could pick out very faint stars just a little to the right of straight ahead for my right eye and a little to the left of straight on for my left eye. The same trick works for trout. Look straight ahead as usual, but be aware of what's slightly off center in your visual field. If you detect any movement or anything that's out of the ordinary, investigate it. Sometimes, sensing a trout with your averted vision is no more than the feeling that something is subtly out of place.

Spotting Motionless Trout

Although trout have to move sooner or later, you may not always want to wait for them. There are ways to spot motionless trout. Concentrate on the shadows that are created by streambed rocks. If most of the rocks are angular, their shadows are, too. If you see a smooth or curved shadow, investigate it—it could be a trout. Check out any shadows that look out of place.

Look for lines that are out of whack. Streams contain a lot of horizontal lines: current lines formed as the water splits around a rock, streambanks, and the edges of fallen trees. Check out any vertical lines you see as you peer into the river; it may just be a stick, or it might be the vertical edge of a trout's tail. Here, too, it pays to use averted vision. Change position now and then; a different angle often reveals a previously invisible trout. Sometimes you may not be able to identify a shape you've spotted even after you move, so you'll have to find yet another angle. Remove your sunglasses to see what the shape looks like in unpolarized light. As a last resort you can wait around to see if the shape moves.

Color will also help you spot motionless trout. A trout's coloration isn't obvious, but you will often get a sense of its presence from a brightness or glow in the water. As you observe more closely, you'll pick up the red along the lateral line of a rainbow trout or the buttery yellow along a brown trout's flanks or the white along the bottom of a brookie's pectoral fins. Color can be an especially important indicator of fish on cloudy days, when diffuse light can intensify the colors and brightness of a trout's subdued hues.

Indirect spotting is another way to see motionless or nearly motionless trout. I learned about this trick from Brian Clarke's and John Goddard's book, *The Trout and the Fly*. It's most useful on very smooth water where you can study surface reflections. Concentrate on straight lines such as the reflection of a tree or the straight side of a rock. Watch the edge of the reflection. If you observe even the slightest blurring of that reflected line, a trout holding close to the surface might have caused it. In still water, a trout's slightest movement can disrupt a reflection.

Spotting a trout indirectly is always exhilarating. It's almost like the trout comes out of a fog and into your mind. One moment you'll be looking at a reflection in the water and the next you will simply *know* that a trout is there.

Riffle Break

Small rectangular or oval slicks known as riffle breaks occur in faster, riffled water. They allow a fisherman to see into the fast water and sometimes spot a trout.

The trout-spotting techniques discussed so far are most useful in fairly slow water. Trout feel a lot safer in riffles, so you should be able to get closer to them than you can in flatter water. A riffle break—a slick piece of water moving downstream through a riffle—gives you a good shot at seeing a trout in faster water. Riffle breaks are usually several square feet in size and oval or rectangular. With polarized lenses you can see clearly to the bottom when you look into a riffle break; if there is a trout there you will see it plain as day. When you're in riffles that include pocket water, look for slicks around rocks that will allow you to see into the water.

Finally, once you've located a trout, take a moment to mark it in relation to the terrain before you move into casting position. There's nothing more frustrating than getting into position only to find that you don't remember where the trout is. Triangulate your fish's location with obvious streamside features such as rocks or trees.

Finding Trout When You Can't Spot Them

One of the great delights of fishing small flies is that the waters where they are most important tend to be clear. With the exception of particularly heavy runoff, brief heavy rainstorms, or large water releases, spring creeks and tailwaters tend to remain clear throughout the year. This condition makes it possible to spot the trout themselves or their riseforms most of the time.

For those occasional times when it is difficult to spot trout, it's best to rely on the same basic reading-the-water rules that you would use on any trout stream. Pay special attention to seams where water of two different speeds come together; troughs or depressions in runs, glides, and riffles; slick water behind rocks, backwater eddies, shelves, and drop-offs; and riffle lines off points. Always remember that the trout are trying to occupy water where they can eat more calories than they use chasing their food.

Finding Trout When You Can't See Them

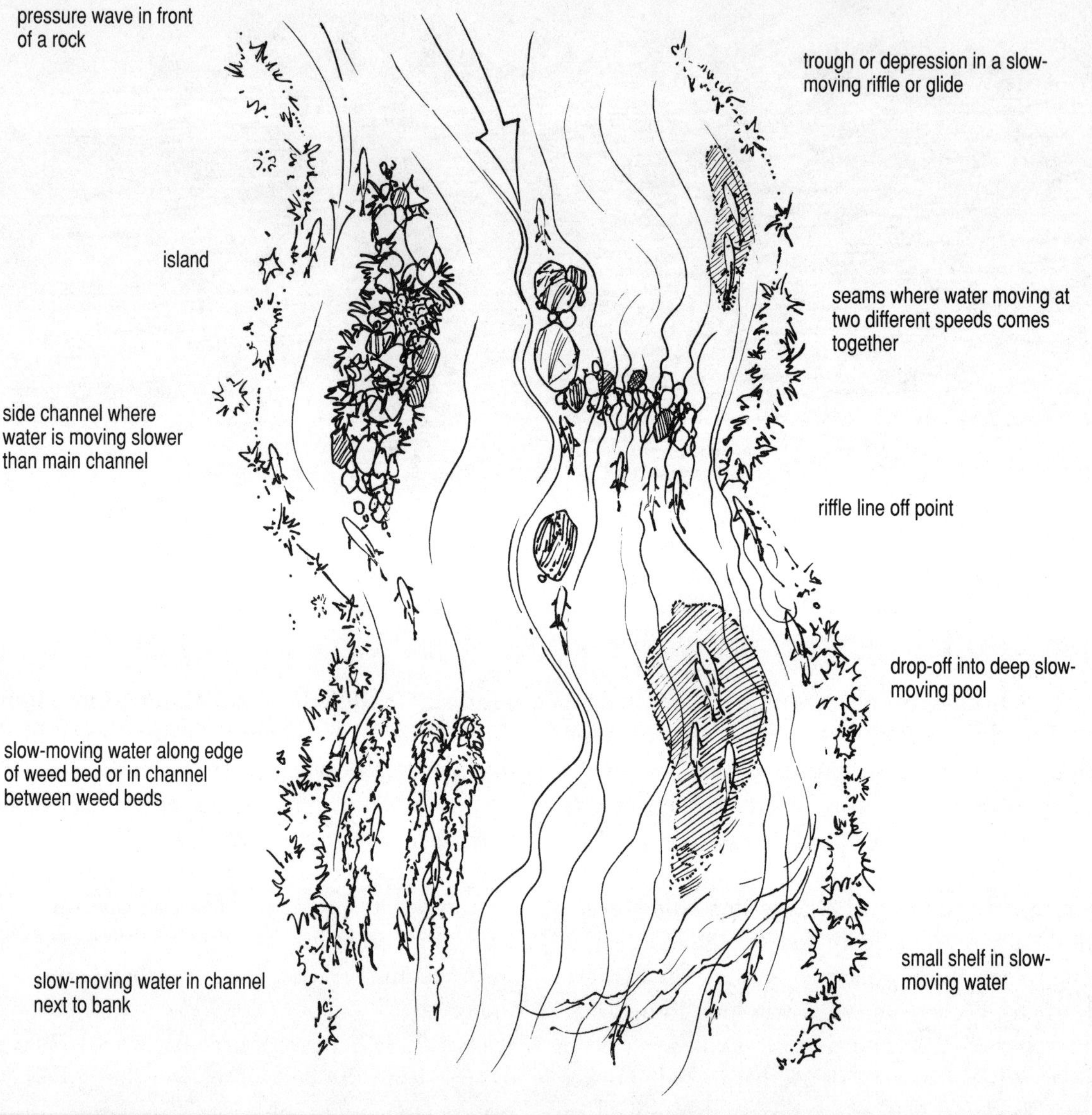

pressure wave in front of a rock

trough or depression in a slow-moving riffle or glide

island

seams where water moving at two different speeds comes together

side channel where water is moving slower than main channel

riffle line off point

drop-off into deep slow-moving pool

slow-moving water along edge of weed bed or in channel between weed beds

slow-moving water in channel next to bank

small shelf in slow-moving water

With that most basic metabolic equation in mind, note that when it comes to small flies, the trout will seek out slower-moving water that offers a steady supply of tiny insects. The slow water requires a small expenditure of energy on the trout's part, which makes it worthwhile to

feed on the smaller insects. It's especially worthwhile when there are a lot of the tiny insects in the drift. Look for slow-moving edge water along the banks, weed beds, riffle lines, and eddies. Pay attention to obvious drop-offs into deep water where trout have slower water, hiding cover, and a supply of food. Also look for the smaller hard-to-see ledges in slow-moving water. All side channels where the current is reduced are likely spots to find trout feeding on small flies.

Developing trout-spotting skills will elevate your small-fly fishing experiences. Spotting a big trout tucked up under a grassy bank that no one else has detected is electric. Putting a stalk on it and successfully presenting a fly is ecstasy. You don't have to spend hours practicing your trout-spotting skills. Work it into your routine. Take a few minutes to study the river before you begin to fish. Once you're on the water and casting, take a break now and then to make observations. Investigate anything that seems out of place. It's that simple. You'll begin to learn; you'll start to see the subtleties. You'll see trout. You'll feel the electricity. . . .

CHAPTER FOUR

Basic Small-Fly Nymphing Techniques

It's dawn on Colorado's renowned Frying Pan River. I'm on a less famous section of the river, but nonetheless a few early bird fly fishers are on the water. Like many western tailwaters and spring creeks, the Frying Pan provides ideal habitat for tiny two-winged insects that fly fishermen know as midges, as well as for the small mayflies such as blue-winged olives and pale morning duns.

I'm on the water early because the largest trout in these productive tailwaters get cagey when lots of fishermen are around. The trick is to be the angler who shows them the first artificial fly of the day. It's often possible to find the trout already in the feeding lanes at first light and methodically picking off midge larvae. That's not surprising either. Most tailwater and spring creek fly fishers know that what midges lack in size they make up for in numbers.

Gary Borger noted that in any given lake or stream at least 50 percent of the insect species are midges. The larvae numbers alone can exceed 50,000 per square yard. Over the years I've observed that the trout in midge-rich rivers such as the Frying Pan will literally feed on them all day long—there always seems to be enough midge larvae and midge pupae drifting in the water to attract their attention.

I've had my eye on one particular trout for the last few mornings. The fish is stationed about a foot off a grassy bank in two feet of slow-moving water. It's suspended about a foot off the stream bottom and the morning light has revealed that it's regularly feeding on something below the water's surface. I can tell that because I see its head move side to side an inch or two, or sometimes I'll catch a bit of a flash in the water, or most tellingly, I will see its mouth open and take something. The regular feeding behavior coupled with the fact that the trout is suspended in the water column is a classic example of sub-surface feeding to an abundant source of small, immature aquatic insects.

I seined the river downstream from the fish and wasn't surprised to find mostly midge larvae and, to a lesser degree, midge pupae. Over the years I've learned that where midges occur I can expect some larvae to be in the drift at almost any time. If a hatch is imminent I expect to see more pupae in the sample. The bottom line is the trout are always on the lookout for immature forms of midges in the drift.

The universal tactic in the West for presenting a subsurface small-fly imitation to trout is what I call the standard dead-drift nymphing presentation. This technique depends on weight attached to the leader to get one or two flies down to the trout. Typically, a strike indicator is used to detect when the trout takes the fly.

As important as dead-drifting is to subsurface small-fly fishing success, I choose a less well-known tactic. I tie a single size 22 Miracle Nymph imitation that has been modified to include a black 2mm tungsten bead to the end of my rather long 3-foot, 6X tippet. I then make a very quiet wakeless wading approach downstream and across from the trout. I get as close to the fish as possible without spooking it.

Once in position I cast the weighted Miracle Nymph far enough upstream from the trout to allow it time to sink. I accomplish this with a slack-producing check cast. As the fly drifts downstream, I lift the rod tip to the point that there is no fly line on the water when the imitation drifts into the trout's strike zone. The leader is the only line I have in the water as the fly drifts by the trout unnoticed. I know all of this because I've positioned myself in such a way that I can watch the trout. If he takes the imitation, I'll see it; watching the trout itself is the ultimate strike indicator.

My luck changes a few presentations later when I see the trout turn a bit to its right and pick the Miracle Nymph out of the drift. I tighten up on the line to make sure I'm hooked up and gently set the hook. You don't need much to embed a size 22 iron. And I'm into the trout.

The fish dogs me close to the bottom for the first minute or so before it realizes it's hooked and then makes two strong runs. I pressure and turn it by first holding my rod low and parallel to the water on the upstream side and then flipping the rod over to the other side of my body low and parallel to the water on the downstream side. In this way I am able to quickly tire, land, and release what turns out to be a 5-pound-plus Yellowstone cutthroat trout.

I used what I call the basic freestyle nymphing technique to catch that Frying Pan River trout. It's a specialized technique that is well suited for fishing subsurface small-fly imitations to trout that are feeding in shallow, slow-moving water. A standard dead-drift presentation was less desirable in this situation because the split shot and strike indicator would have been too disruptive on the calm water surface and might have spooked the fish.

My small-fly nymphing success on that trout was the product of a series of observations and decisions that culminated with the first cast. I had to spot the trout first and then determine if he

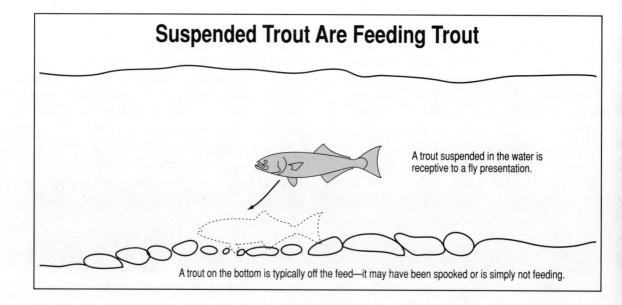

Suspended Trout Are Feeding Trout

A trout suspended in the water is receptive to a fly presentation.

A trout on the bottom is typically off the feed—it may have been spooked or is simply not feeding.

was feeding. I did that by carefully observing the trout's behavior. This trout was easy because I was able to see it open its mouth and feed. But the fish also displayed more subtle feeding indicators. The most basic indicator was that the fish was suspended in the water. A trout that is laying low on the stream bottom is often off the feed. Even if a suspended trout isn't actively feeding, it's a sign that with a proper presentation you may still get a strike. The movement of the trout's head back and forth in the current and the obvious opening of its mouth clearly indicated that it was actively feeding on something drifting in the current. The occasional flash was just more evidence.

The next step, especially if you're new to a river or new to nymphing with small flies, is to get a sample of what's in the drift. That isn't always possible, but if you can do it, you'll learn plenty about what's going on. Be sure to get far enough downstream to assure that the trout will not spook. It's important to fine-tune your sam-

ple by taking it from the same current line that the trout is holding in. That means if the fish is up against the opposite bank, take your sample there; if it's in a little riffle a third of the way out from the bank, try to take your sample downstream from that. And remember that when it comes to midges in the drift, you'd better have a pretty fine mesh on your seine!

Once you have an idea of what the trout are feeding on, select an imitation, but before you tie it on the tippet, a decision must be made about the most suitable technique to fish it with. If the trout is feeding in faster, deep water, a standard dead-drift nymphing technique is suitable. Slow-moving water harboring spooky trout may require freestyle nymphing tactics or a variation of standard dead-drift nymphing techniques. When you decide on what technique to use, do any necessary re-rigging *before* you move to your casting position. You want to be all set once you're in place to make the first cast.

A strike indicator isn't used when freestyle nymphing.

Next, try to find a casting position that will allow you to make a drag-free presentation. The closer you can get, the better the chance of accomplishing this. Only experience can teach you how close you can get without spooking the fish. Expect that fish in shallow, calm water will be more difficult to approach than those in deep, heavier water. An approach from straight downstream may get you closer than an upstream-and-across approach. Once you decide on your casting position, try to cause as little disruption as possible when you wade into it.

SMALL-FLY FREESTYLE NYMPHING

Freestyle nymphing isn't as new as it sounds. It's actually the way that many of us learned how to fish larger nymph imitations. We later applied that knowledge to fishing small flies with a tiny split shot attached to the leader before strike indicators were in widespread use. Most recent innovations for weighting tiny flies have made pure freestyle nymphing techniques available to small-fly fishermen.

The important elements of the small-fly basic freestyle nymphing technique are:

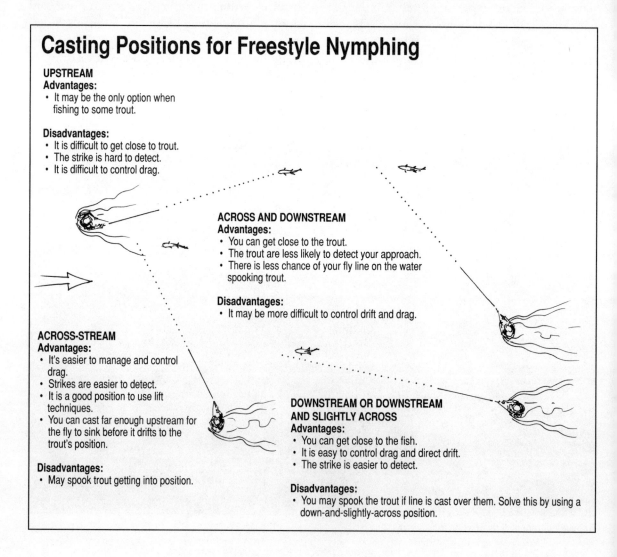

Casting Positions for Freestyle Nymphing

UPSTREAM
Advantages:
• It may be the only option when fishing to some trout.

Disadvantages:
• It is difficult to get close to trout.
• The strike is hard to detect.
• It is difficult to control drag.

ACROSS AND DOWNSTREAM
Advantages:
• You can get close to the trout.
• The trout are less likely to detect your approach.
• There is less chance of your fly line on the water spooking trout.

Disadvantages:
• It may be more difficult to control drift and drag.

ACROSS-STREAM
Advantages:
• It's easier to manage and control drag.
• Strikes are easier to detect.
• It is a good position to use lift techniques.
• You can cast far enough upstream for the fly to sink before it drifts to the trout's position.

Disadvantages:
• May spook trout getting into position.

DOWNSTREAM OR DOWNSTREAM AND SLIGHTLY ACROSS
Advantages:
• You can get close to the fish.
• It is easy to control drag and direct drift.
• The strike is easier to detect.

Disadvantages:
• You may spook the trout if line is cast over them. Solve this by using a down-and-slightly-across position.

Get Close to Feeding Trout

Find a downstream (or downstream-and-slightly-across), across-and-downstream, across-stream, or upstream casting position in that order of preference. If you can stay on the bank without wading at all, do it. Get as close to the feeding trout as possible. This will allow you, with the help of a good pair of sunglasses, to observe the trout and see it take the fly. If you can't see the trout you will still be close enough to watch where the leader and water intersect. Use that intersection as your strike indicator. If the leader stops, hesitates, or does anything out of the ordinary, gently lift the rod. If you feel a fish on, set the hook; if you don't feel a fish, lower the tip and continue the drift.

Getting close to the fish allows you to keep the fly line off the water. As the fly drifts toward you, lift the rod higher and higher off the water to manage slack. It will also give you a natural drift and allow you to detect strikes more easily. If you need to make a somewhat longer cast and some fly line ends up on the surface, use the juncture where the butt of the leader and fly line are joined as a strike indicator.

The secret to successful freestyle nymphing and some dead-drift nymphing styles is not often clearly taught to beginners. If you're not using a strike indicator, it is crucial that you keep the slack line off the water and the rod tip high. For many years I thought that keeping the tip up and the slack out was mainly to help with strike detection. That is indeed true, but keeping the rod tip up also suspends the fly just a bit as it drifts, and that's what makes it act like the real thing. It also helps prevent snagging the stream bottom.

The closer you can get to the trout, the better your chances are of getting a natural drift with freestyle techniques. That's why some people called it *short-line* nymphing when I first started nymphing thirty-five years ago.

Use a Weighted Fly to Match the Naturals

Recently, very fine wires, small brass and tungsten beads (1.5mm and 2mm), and the availability of small hooks made of heavier standard-size wires have made it possible to make weighted flies as small as size 24 or even size 26. Most fly fishers tie the tiny weighted flies to the tippet with a clinch knot. Tie the fly on with a tiny single surgeon's loop if you feel the clinch knot is impeding its action.

Use a Long, Light Tippet

I usually use a 5X or 6X tippet when I freestyle nymph with small flies. Sometimes a very lightly weighted small fly will have trouble breaking through the surface tension. I've found that lengthening a nylon tippet to 3 feet or more will usually solve the problem, and more importantly, it gives the fly a better action under the surface. Of course, if getting the fly down becomes a problem, you can switch to fluorocarbon, which will break through the surface tension and sink a little better.

I often use freestyle nymphing techniques to fish to large trout that are in shallow, slow water near the banks. If it doesn't spook the fish, I like fishing an imitation weighted with a bright gold, silver, or copper bead because I can often visually track the fly as it drifts downstream toward the trout. That way I know for sure that I got the drift right. Small-fly freestyle techniques are also effective in shallow riffles, seams, and the shallow slicks behind rocks. If you find that the trout are sensitive to the flashy metallic bead, switch to a fly where the weight is hidden under the dubbing.

Occasionally, you'll find that the tiny splash of a small beadhead or weighted fly will spook the trout. If the fish is close in to the bank, try casting the fly lightly up on the bank and pulling it into the water. Your options will be limited if the trout is farther out in the stream. Sometimes it's possible to cast farther upstream without scaring the trout, but be prepared to help the tiny

Surgeon's Loop with Small Fly

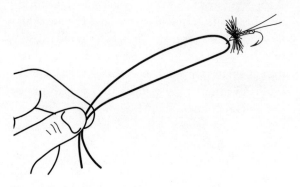

Thread fly onto leader; then form a single loop.

Form a second loop in the doubled-over leader material.

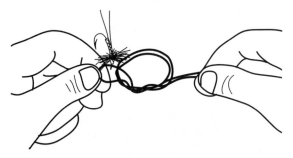

Carefully pass the single loop with the fly through the double loop one time. (Most instructions for a surgeon's loop recommend passing the single loop through the double loop twice, but once is usually enough for small flies. If you find that the loop slips, go to a double loop.)

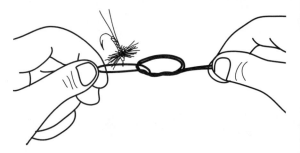

Tighten the loop by pulling on the single loop of fly while holding the other ends of the leader material in your opposite hand.

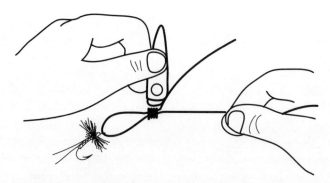

Trim tag end of the tippet material as close as possible to the knot without nicking the coils. *Illustrations derived from* The Orvis Fly-Fishing Guide.

nymph's drift with a minilift here and there to get it over a rock or with a mid-drift correction with the rod tip to get it in front of the trout. You might also be able to cast the fly into a nearby riffle or seam to cover the splash.

As a rule, a dead-drift presentation is best, but I do fool around with lifts once in a while. The well-known English nymphers G. E. M. Skues and later Frank Sawyer along with the American James Leisenring perfected the art of lifting a subsurface fly in front of feeding trout. They fished the nymph much like a dry fly by actually spotting feeding trout under the surface, casting a weighted fly upstream of the trout, allowing the fly to sink, and then gently lifting it in front of the trout as it drifted by. The movement often triggered an exciting strike.

You will have to be in an across-and-downstream or across-stream casting position to make most lifts. I don't get very fancy with it either. I just smoothly and slowly lift the tip of the rod either when I see the fly a few feet in front of the trout or when I figure it's about in that position. Sometimes all it takes is a twitch. If a trout is responsive to lifts or twitches you'll see it move immediately to the fly when you apply the action. Once again, it pays to be close when attempting lifts. You'll have a chance of seeing the fly or at least seeing the trout, and you'll have much better control over the lift.

I reserve the upstream casting position for when all my other options are depleted. It's not that I can't make an effective drag-free presentation from upstream, but rather that my chances of spooking the trout increase dramatically during the approach. I most often use the upstream approach for trout that are feeding close in to the bank. The key is to mark the trout's location in relation to a streamside landmark, move well back from the bank, and then walk far enough upstream to remain undetected when you move back toward the stream. Once I'm next to the water, I crouch and sneak down toward the fish

as close as I dare. The odds are that I won't get close enough to see the trout, but I know its location because I can see where I marked it.

I then strip enough line off the reel for the cast *and* to feed line downstream as the fly drifts to the trout. The trick is to make the cast short enough to not spook the fish and then feed out slack with S curves of line. Strike detection can be problematical. Watch the leader–fly line connection closely and be sure to hold the fly line between your thumb and forefinger because you may be able to feel the strike. Also, closely watch the water's surface. Sometimes you will get an inadvertent lift when fishing the nymph downstream, and you'll see a little surface disturbance when the trout takes the fly.

If you think a straight downstream cast will spook the trout, consider making a short across-and-downstream cast and then allowing it to swing into the proper drift lane upstream from the trout. If you throw a few feet of slack into the line on the swing and hold the rod tip toward the water, it may dampen any surface disturbance caused when the line swings in the current. Once the fly has swung into position upstream of the trout, feed out S curves the same as you would do on a downstream presentation.

You may want to experiment with the tuck cast for certain small-fly freestyle nymphing situations. Joe Humphreys introduced the tuck cast in his book *Trout Tactics*. Joe and George Harvey designed this upstream or upstream-and-across cast to create enough slack in the line to get a weighted nymph to the bottom before drag on the fly line affects it. Although the tuck cast works best for fishing larger weighted nymphs in anywhere from moderately moving to fast-moving water, you may find it useful when you need a bit more slack to get a small fly down deeper. In most small-fly nymphing situations, it will be necessary to add weight to the leader about 8 to 12 inches above a single fly because it's difficult to weight a small fly enough to successfully make

Across and Downstream Freestyle Nymphing

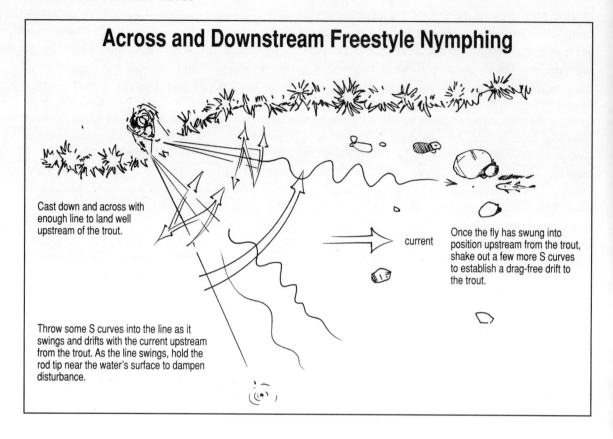

Cast down and across with enough line to land well upstream of the trout.

current

Once the fly has swung into position upstream from the trout, shake out a few more S curves to establish a drag-free drift to the trout.

Throw some S curves into the line as it swings and drifts with the current upstream from the trout. As the line swings, hold the rod tip near the water's surface to dampen disturbance.

a tuck cast (see the seciton on small-fly dead-drift nymphing for details on using weight on the leader).

To execute this cast, stop the rod sharply at the 11 o'clock position of the forward cast with the last two fingers of the casting hand pulling the rod toward you while at the same time using the thumb to push it forward. This snap will overpower the loop, causing the weight and small fly to bounce back and tuck under the line. The fly will be propelled into the water with enough slack to allow it to get to the stream bottom before drag on the line lifts it. The fly usually makes a bit of a splash when it hits the surface, so you may want to cast a little farther upstream than you would in slower or shallower water.

As the fly drifts toward you, lift the rod tip higher to manage slack line and drag the same way you do for a standard freestyle nymphing presentation. Strikes are detected by watching the fish or the leader and water interface. For longer casts with some fly line on the water, watch the juncture between the fly line and leader butt to detect strikes.

SMALL-FLY DEAD-DRIFT NYMPHING
If you have trouble detecting strikes, need to make longer casts, or are fishing heavier water, try using dead-drift nymphing tactics with a small-fly twist.

Most fly fishers are familiar with basic dead-drift nymphing techniques. Dead-drift nymphing as it's known today was developed on Rocky Mountain tailwaters and freestone rivers in the 1960s. Its popularity has since spread throughout much of the country. A basic all-around dead-

Small-fly dead-drift nymphing employs a strike indicator, and weight is attached to the leader.

drift nymphing rig uses just enough weight attached to the leader to get one or two flies to the stream bottom and allow them to drift downstream in a natural fashion. A strike indicator is often attached 1½ to 2 times the depth of the water being fished above the weight. Although the weight attached to the leader bounces along the bottom as the rig drifts downstream, it should be noted that a floating-style strike indicator (hard foam, open-cell foam, yarn) does provide some buoyancy to the nymph imitations. This little bit of extra buoyancy when coupled with good line-mending practices presents the flies in a more natural manner and lessens the chances of snagging the bottom.

When I learned to dead-drift nymph, no one used strike indicators. We attached a split shot to the leader that was heavy enough to get the un-

weighted nymph imitations to the bottom but still bounce downstream along the bottom in a natural fashion. We dead-drifted the nymphs on a short line in a fashion very similar to a freestyle nymphing technique except there was weight attached to the leader and we didn't use a tuck cast. Strikes were detected by watching the intersection of the leader and the water or the trout itself. If the leader stopped, hesitated, moved upstream, or acted out of the ordinary in any way, I set the hook. At first I hooked the bottom a lot, but over time I learned what a real strike looked like.

I switched over to strike indicators for most of my dead-drift nymphing when they became popular because they allowed me to make longer casts and, like most fly fishers at the time, I thought they helped me pick up on more strikes.

As it turned out, I'm not sure I saw any more strikes, but I do think that I detected the strikes sooner when I used an indicator. That meant more solid hookups. In addition, watching the buoyant strike indicator helped me determine if I was getting a drag-free drift—if the indicator dragged on the surface, it was a good indication that my nymph imitations were not drifting in a natural fashion below the water's surface.

Nonetheless, with all the advantages strike indicators offer, I would still recommend that anyone who is serious about dead-drift nymphing with small flies first learn the technique without a strike indicator. I believe that nymphing without the indicator will make you a lot more aware of very subtle signs that indicate a strike. You'll learn how to feel an almost subliminal change of the fly line in your hand when you get a strike. It will also force you to observe the trout more closely for a hint of a flash or a turn of the head that may indicate a strike. Over time your sense of these subtle indicators will become ingrained to the degree that they almost become subconscious. It's almost like you see or sense the take, it goes straight to your arm, and you set the hook. It totally bypasses your conscious, reasoning mind. And that's what you want because it puts you on the strike a few milliseconds sooner, which are a few milliseconds less time that the trout has to reject the imitation.

I found that when I began experimenting with and using strike indicators, I still employed all the instincts that I'd developed when I didn't use them. Whenever possible, I still watch the trout rather that the indicator, for example. I wonder if nymphers who have always used indicators do that. My point is that fishing small flies is a subtle, delicate art. In its purest form it comes down to a bare minimum of finely tuned tools and techniques, aided by razor sharp instinct. And with practice you can hone your instincts in the same way that practice improves your casting.

TACKLE REFINEMENTS FOR SMALL-FLY NYMPHING

The rod of choice for small-fly freestyle and dead-drift nymphing on larger water is graphite, 9 feet long and for a 3-weight to 5-weight floating fly line. I would recommend a moderately fast graphite that is a little tippy. That will give you enough speed in the tip to set up quickly, but it won't be so stiff that you break the tippet when the trout pulls back. If you prefer bamboo, go with an 8- to 8½-foot rod with an action that stays toward the tip.

Strike Indicators

Most nymphers use buoyant indicators now. They are typically made from hard or soft foam, yarn, or putty. More than any other nymphing innovation, it is the buoyant strike indicator that has extended the range of effective dead-drift nymphing. The indicator actually provides enough buoyancy to allow the weight to bounce naturally along the stream bottom. A properly mended nymphing rig using a strike indicator will allow long drag-free drifts. All but straight upstream long-line dead-drift nymphing presentations made without an indicator quickly encounter drag on the fly line even when the line is mended.

There are a number of types of strike indicators available to nymph fishermen. Not all of them are appropriate for nymphing with small flies, though.

Less is best for small-fly strike indicators. A tiny stick-on indicator *(left)*, strike putty rubbed over a leader knot *(center)*, or a disposable stick-on strike indicator that has been cut in half are all good options for small-fly nymphing styles.

Strike putty has several advantages for small-fly fishermen. It's best to form it around a leader knot.

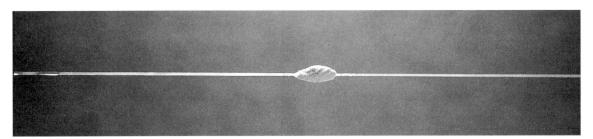

Strike putty formed around a leader knot will stay in place better.

The indicator can be used when the weight attached to the leader is intended to bounce along the bottom or when an imitation is meant to be suspended from the indicator above the stream bottom. I usually use yarn indicators trimmed down to a smaller size or soft disposable foam pinch–on indicators trimmed to the smallest usable size.

The big, clunky, hard foam with broken toothpick holder-style indicators should be reserved for the heaviest, deepest waters where they won't spook the fish. Moldable putty-type

indicators are buoyant if you add enough, but I prefer to use the putty as a smaller, less obtrusive indicator when I'm fishing nymphs or pupae in the film. Also remember that a dry fly can be used as a strike indicator as long as it's large enough to not be pulled under by the weight attached to the leader or a weighted fly.

A less common category is strike indicators that sink. These include a bright section of Amnesia tied into the leader as a butt section or a little sleeve of fluorescent orange fly line threaded on to the leader and pushed up against a knot somewhere in the butt section of the leader. This style of indicator was a popular crossover between using no indicator at all and buoyant-type indicators. Once in a while they are useful if a buoyant-type indicator disrupts the surface too much, but if that's the case, it's probably best to switch over to freestyle techniques. The common practice was to put them in right at the nail knot between the fly line and leader, which wasn't really practical if you didn't want your fly line to get on the water when you were short-line nymphing. I moved them down into the interior of the butt section of the leader where I could still see them under the water. My friend Roger Hill took the leader-born strike indicator a step further by painting all the knots on his hand-tied leaders a fluorescent orange.

Weight

Lead split shot comes in very small sizes that are applicable to even the slowest-moving water, but it can be a pain to get off the leader once it's been attached. Shot with tabs that allow you to easily take it off is available but only in larger sizes. If you need a lot of weight, ribbon-style lead or lead sleeves are available.

My favorite weighting material for slow- to moderate-moving water is soft lead putty or most recently the nontoxic lead-free putty alternatives. I can use exactly how much I need, and it's easy to put on and take off the leader. The downside is that you can cast it off if you're really whipping the rod around, but since most of my small-fly nymphing takes place close in and is delicate in nature, that often isn't a problem. If you do have trouble with it flinging off, try forming it around a knot in the leader, or for heavier water form it around a split shot. The putty can be easily removed or added if conditions change, rather than taking the harder-to-remove split shot off.

Sooner or later lead is going to be banned, and that will make things a little tough for small-

A split shot can be difficult to remove from the leader once it has been attached. Try using a shot that is lighter than required.

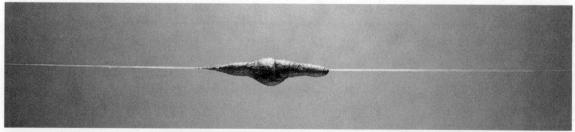

And then form weighted putty in a tapered shape around the shot. The weighted putty is easier to add and remove than shot, and the tapered shape snags less on the stream bottom. In addition, the shot helps hold the weighted putty in place on the leader.

fly fishers. Many of the alternatives now available are bulky and difficult to work with. Thankfully, nontoxic weighting putty is available. Hopefully, additional options will present themselves as the need arises.

FISHING THE SMALL-FLY DEAD-DRIFT NYMPHING RIG
Casting

Beginning dead-drift nymph fishermen quickly learn that they must modify their casting style. Forget about that beautiful tight loop you worked so hard to achieve for your dry-fly fishing. A dead-drift nymphing rig is full of hinges. There's one at the strike indicator and one where the weight is attached to the leader. Many nymphers use a modified roll cast. When the drift is complete they allow the nymphing rig to swing directly downstream from them, raise the rod tip, which brings the weight to the surface,

and then use the surface tension created to water-load the rod and punch out a forward cast. The water load completely eliminates the need for an aerial backcast.

If conditions prohibit water loading, use a standard fly cast but modify it by first slowing down and smoothing out the backcast. You must allow enough time for the weight and strike indicator to straighten out on the backcast. Any jerkiness in the cast will cause the leader to rotate around the hinge point and tangle. When the backcast is complete, open the loop on the forward cast. If you do have a little bit of wobble around a hinge point, the open loop will prevent the fly or flies from tangling. And remember that as tempting as it is to make longer casts, always opt for the shortest cast possible. The more line there is in the air the more there is that can go wrong!

Once the cast is completed, the fly line will have to be mended to get the longest possible

No-lead, nontoxic weighted putty is now available. It's especially useful when fishing small flies.

Short-Line Dead-Drift Nymphing Casts: The Water-Load Cast

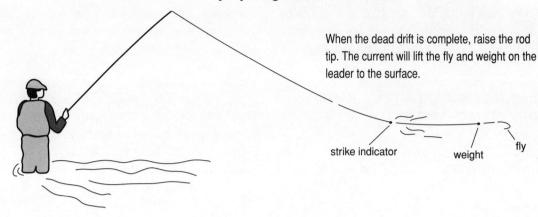

When the dead drift is complete, raise the rod tip. The current will lift the fly and weight on the leader to the surface.

strike indicator   weight   fly

A water-load cast uses the current instead of a backcast to load the fly rod. It's a good way to make short casts when dead-drift nymphing because the fly, weight, and strike indicator will tangle less on the forward cast.

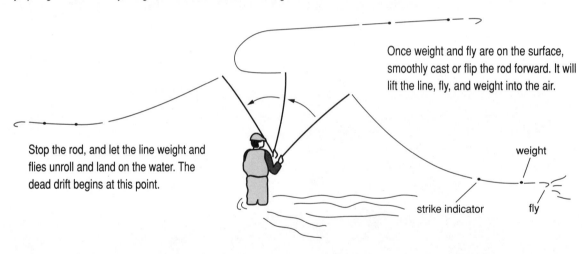

Once weight and fly are on the surface, smoothly cast or flip the rod forward. It will lift the line, fly, and weight into the air.

Stop the rod, and let the line weight and flies unroll and land on the water. The dead drift begins at this point.

weight

strike indicator   fly

drag-free drift. Depending on the speed of the water being fished, a single long drift may require multiple mends. A good rule of thumb when casting across and upstream is that the strike indicator should always go first downstream. If the fly line begins to form that classic drag-producing downstream U, flip it upstream of the strike indicator. With practice, mending causes little disturbance to the indicator, and even if it does, you're better off than if the flies are dragging in the current. I've actually gotten strikes when the fly jerked upstream a smidgen during a mend.

Remember, too, that as weird as it is to cast a dead-drift rig, you will still have to be accurate, especially when casting to fish that you've spotted. Trout feeding below the surface on small nymphs, larvae, and pupae are notorious for not moving very far to pick off the morsels. Don't be fooled into thinking that where your strike indicator hits the water is where your imitations are. Watch for the little splash caused by the weight. The flies will drift downstream in a line from that splash. Better yet, get close enough to see the flies as they drift downstream. The most common mistake I ob-

A Dead-Drift Nymphing Rig

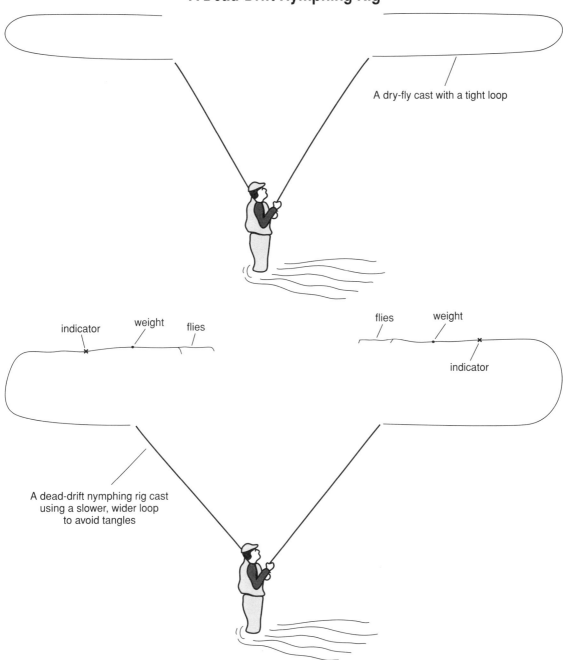

A dry-fly cast with a tight loop

indicator   weight   flies

flies   weight

indicator

A dead-drift nymphing rig cast
using a slower, wider loop
to avoid tangles

The dead-drift nymphing rig has hinges at the indicator and weight. To keep from tangling, you must cast a wider loop. Open up the casting and slow down the line speed a bit. On the backcast, wait for the line to straighten and then bring the rod smoothly forward. At the end of the forward casting stroke, smoothly lower the rod tip. Avoid stopping the rod abruptly at the end of the forward casting stroke.

Dead-Drift Nymphing: Mending Line

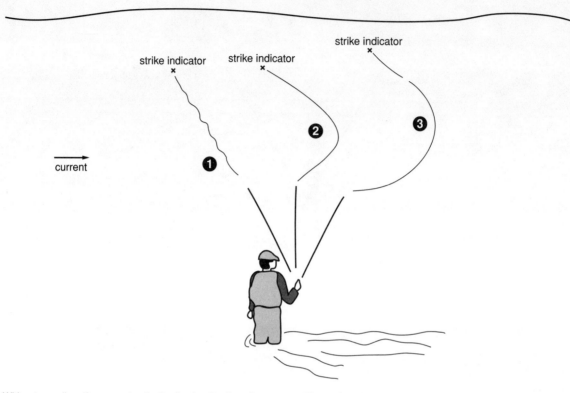

Without mending, the current pulls the floating line in a downstream U, causing the nymph imitation to pull up from the bottom and move at an unnatural speed.

Underwater View

1. Flies bounce downstream in a natural fashion when weight is under the indicator fly.
2. As drag begins to affect the floating fly line, flies lift from the bottom. The indicator is now drifting ahead of the weight.
3. Flies are well up off of the bottom, moving in an unnatural fashion. The weight is dragging behind the indicator.

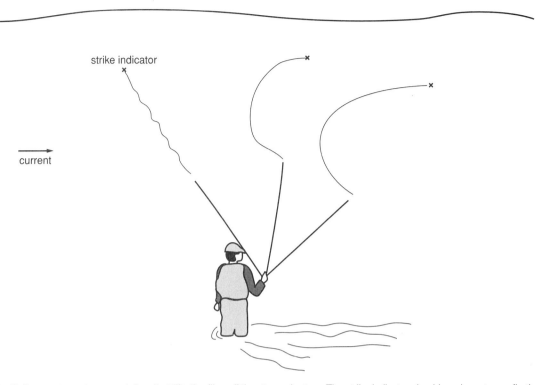

strike indicator

current

Mend the fly line upstream to prevent drag that lifts the flies off the stream bottom. The strike indicator should go downstream first!

Basic Two-Fly Inline Dead-Drift Nymphing Rigs

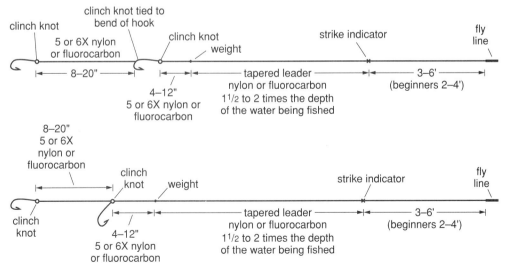

clinch knot

clinch knot tied to
bend of hook

clinch knot

5 or 6X nylon
or fluorocarbon

weight

strike indicator

fly
line

8–20"

4–12"
5 or 6X nylon or
fluorocarbon

tapered leader
nylon or fluorocarbon
1½ to 2 times the depth
of the water being fished

3–6'
(beginners 2–4')

8–20"
5 or 6X
nylon or
fluorocarbon

clinch
knot

weight

strike indicator

fly
line

clinch
knot

4–12"
5 or 6X nylon
or fluorocarbon

tapered leader
nylon or fluorocarbon
1½ to 2 times the depth
of the water being fished

3–6'
(beginners 2–4')

Notes: A tapered leader isn't crucial for a nymphing-only rig, but it will allow you to switch over to dry flies or other unweighted presentation styles more easily. Fluorocarbon leader material is most important from the weight to the flies.

served while guiding fly fishermen new to dead-drift nymphing was that they didn't know where their fly was in relation to the fish.

I most often find myself using two flies when dead-drift nymphing small flies, but I will fish a single fly if I'm confident about what the trout are taking because it tangles less. If you're new to nymphing small flies you may want to start with a single-fly rig until you get the hang of it.

For two-fly rigs I like to tie the flies in line. The first fly is tied to the tippet with a clinch knot, and the second, which is sometimes called the point fly, is attached to the first by a section of tippet material. This dropper line can be tied with a clinch knot to the first fly at the bend of the hook or through the eye. You can add weight anywhere from 4 to 10 inches above the first fly.

The section of tippet material used to connect the flies in a two-fly inline nymphing rig can be tied with a clinch knot to the eye of the first fly or

. . . it may be tied with a clinch knot to the bend of the first fly.

TYING A CLINCH KNOT LOOP

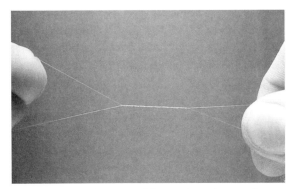

1. Form a loop of tippet material around your last two fingers by wrapping the tag end of the tippet five or six times around the main length of tippet.

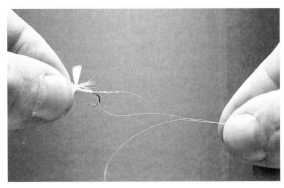

4. Place loop in hook bend.

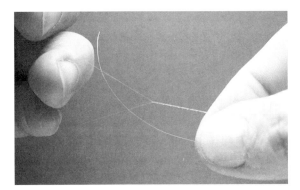

2. Pass the tag end through the loop.

5. Pull the main length of tippet to tighten loop on hook bend.

3. Remove fingers from loop.

6. Trim tag end.

Two-Fly Nymphing Rigs: The Relationship of Weight Placement and Fly Position and Action

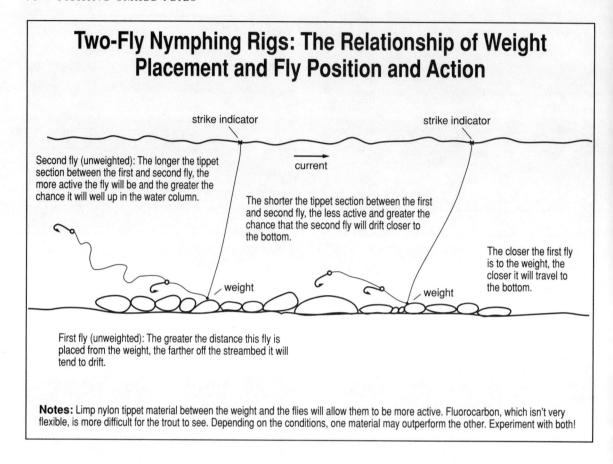

strike indicator

strike indicator

Second fly (unweighted): The longer the tippet section between the first and second fly, the more active the fly will be and the greater the chance it will well up in the water column.

current

The shorter the tippet section between the first and second fly, the less active and greater the chance that the second fly will drift closer to the bottom.

The closer the first fly is to the weight, the closer it will travel to the bottom.

weight

weight

First fly (unweighted): The greater the distance this fly is placed from the weight, the farther off the streambed it will tend to drift.

Notes: Limp nylon tippet material between the weight and the flies will allow them to be more active. Fluorocarbon, which isn't very flexible, is more difficult for the trout to see. Depending on the conditions, one material may outperform the other. Experiment with both!

Small-Fly Dead-Drift Nymphing Rigs

The key to modifying the standard dead-drift nymphing rig for small flies is the arrangement of the flies and the weight. When you don't see any specific feeding activity, try a small-fly attractor rig. Use a larger attractor fly such as a San Juan Worm or Gold-Ribbed Hare's Ear as the first fly. Place the weight 4 or 5 inches above the attractor to keep it close to the bottom. Then tie on 14 to 24 inches of tippet material and add a point fly. The point fly should imitate the most common small-fly species found in the waters being fished—such as a midge pupa or larva or maybe a blue-winged olive or pale morning dun nymph.

The longer the section of tippet between the flies, the more active the point fly will be in the water, which will provide the illusion of an emerging insect. I've found that the trout will often be attracted to the larger dropper fly but will attack the small fly that is actively welling up in the current.

If you notice that trout are stacking up in the feeding lanes or darting and flashing under the water's surface, then a hatch is imminent. Odds are that the trout are feeding on pupae or nymphs ascending from the streambed to the surface. Seine the water to find out what the fish are taking, and try to use two patterns that closely match the naturals but are not identical to each other.

Two-Fly Stealth Dead-Drift Nymphing Rig

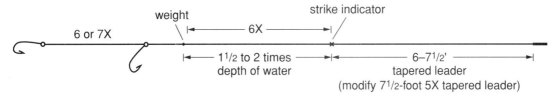

Note: Highly flexible, limp nylon leader material in higher X designations gives small flies a more natural action when used from the strike indicator down. The stealth rig tends to tangle more when cast, so get as close to the trout as possible. Although fluorocarbon is less flexible than soft nylon, it can also be effective in the stealth rig when used at higher X values.

Attach the weight 4 to 10 inches from the dropper fly, depending on how close you want it to drift to the bottom, and then place the point fly 15 to 24 inches from the top fly.

The important thing to remember is to use an imitation of a natural that the trout are looking for *where* the trout are looking for it. If the fish are suspended midway up in the water, use a longer section of tippet between the two flies to allow the point fly to rise more, and put the weight a little farther up the leader from the first (dropper) fly. If the trout are picking off midge larvae near the bottom, shorten the tippet length between the two flies and put the weight closer to the first fly.

If you need to get the point fly down even more, you can put a bit of weight *between* the two flies. The key is to make observations and act accordingly—midges and small mayfly nymphs are often so abundant that the trout will not move much to take a fly. You must get your imitation where they are looking for it.

In heavily fished tailwaters where trout are especially wary, you can further refine the dead-drift nymphing rig by using 6X or lighter tippet material from the strike indicator down to the point fly. Whether the fine tippet material is more difficult for the trout to see is debatable, but the

lighter, limp material will certainly allow the flies to drift in a more natural drag-free fashion.

Finally, there is a crossover point between freestyle and dead-drift nymphing techniques. Instead of weight on the leader, you can use a weighted fly in the dropper position. For small flies this approach is most effective in slow to moderate water speeds because it's difficult to add much weight on a small fly, but a larger attractor dropper fly coupled with a small point fly can be used if more weight is required. A weighted dropper fly rig can be fished using freestyle tactics without a strike indicator or using dead-drift nymphing techniques with an indicator.

SUSPENSION DEAD-DRIFT NYMPHING

If the trout are suspended and feeding regularly at the same level in deeper water, it may be more effective to use a suspension nymphing rig. A suspension rig is made by tying your leader to the strike indicator (I use a yarn indicator with an O-ring or a dry-fly imitation large enough to float the suspended fly) with a clinch knot. Use another clinch knot to tie a section of tippet material at a right angle down from the indicator or to the hook bend. The length of the tippet mate-

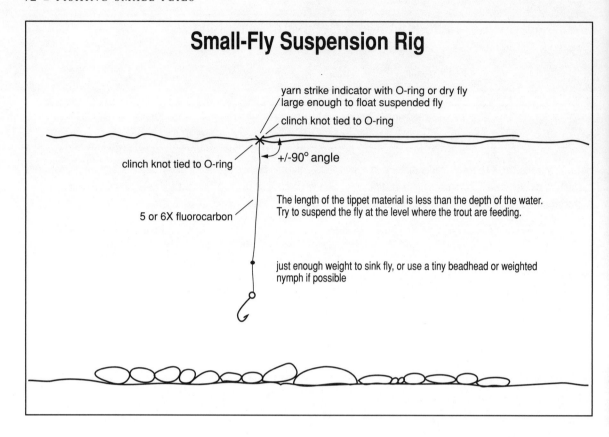

Small-Fly Suspension Rig

yarn strike indicator with O-ring or dry fly large enough to float suspended fly

clinch knot tied to O-ring

clinch knot tied to O-ring

+/-90° angle

5 or 6X fluorocarbon

The length of the tippet material is less than the depth of the water. Try to suspend the fly at the level where the trout are feeding.

just enough weight to sink fly, or use a tiny beadhead or weighted nymph if possible

rial should correspond to the depth where the trout are suspended. Tie a fly to match the naturals at this level. A small weight can be attached to the tippet to get the flies down, or use a weighted imitation.

The advantage of the suspension rig is that it's holding the fly where the trout are looking for food for the entire drift. Also, there's no weight bouncing along the bottom between you and the trout, so strikes are easier to detect. The disadvantage is that the suspension rig is difficult to cast. Try to keep the casts as short as possible.

DEAD-DRIFT SWINGS AND LIFTS

It's almost always best to dead-drift the nymph imitations when weight is attached to the leader, but if you notice that you're getting strikes when

the flies swing at the end of the drift or when you lift the flies out of the water to cast them, incorporate that into your presentation. Always do what the trout tell you to do! If you're getting strikes on a dragged fly, by all means drag the fly! It could be that the dragged fly is imitating microcaddis that are on egg-laying dive bomb runs, or maybe strong swimming *Baetis* nymphs are ascending to the surface. In any event, seine the water, match the hatch, and drag the fly!

It's impossible to overemphasize how important subsurface tactics are to the small-fly angler. Try to develop proficiency at as many of the techniques as possible. That basic proficiency will give you the tools you need to modify the techniques for special situations. Adaptation is the key to successful small-fly fishing, and the broader your knowledge of small-fly techniques, tactics, and flies, the better your chances of successfully meeting new challenges.

Consider that in a productive tailwater such as the Frying Pan River, a trout can easily eat a hundred or more midge pupae or larvae an hour. If you can get your imitation in front of the trout, where it's looking for the natural, you have a good shot at a hookup. And don't forget that there are so many midges in that environment that even the largest trout feed on them.

CHAPTER FIVE

Basic Dry-Fly and In-the-Film Small-Fly Techniques

It's winter 1978, and I'm trying to catch trout that are rising to a hatch of midges on Colorado's South Platte River. I've been fishing the Platte seriously for three years, which means I've been fishing small flies seriously for three years. Tiny insects are a way of life on this water. Here's the problem. I know I've got the right fly on because it's the same pattern the guy upstream from me has on. I went up and asked him what he was using after he landed his fifth or sixth trout, and he was kind enough to give me a few copies of the pattern from his own fly box. So, yeah, I have the right fly on. But I'm not doing squat. I decide to sit down and watch the guy.

The first thing I notice is that he doesn't fish like I do. He's crouched over a bit and casting down-and-across to the dimpling trout. Just as his line and leader straighten over the water, he gracefully sweeps his rod upstream. When the fly and fly line gently land on the water's surface, he drops the rod tip and follows the fly's downstream drift with it. (I'll learn much later that this is what they call a reach cast.) When a trout takes the fly, he lifts the rod tip, tightens up, and imparts an almost imperceptible strike. . . .

It occurs to me that maybe there's more to this than having the right fly. Maybe it's what you do with the fly that matters.

A lot of water has gone down the river since 1978, but I'm still fishing small flies and I believe even more strongly today that small-fly tactics, technique, and style are at least as important to small-fly fishing success as the fly pattern you present. Every time I run into a dry-fly fishing situation involving small flies, whether it's familiar or new to me, I've learned to evaluate it by remembering three words: observe, assess, present.

I always find myself coming back to the importance of observation when fishing small flies. It's hard to explain to some fishermen, but you may be more successful by *not* fishing for a few minutes when you first get on the water or when fishing conditions change. Take time to get an idea of what the trout are doing and come up with a plan before you start casting. It's important to all small-fly fishing, but it's absolutely crucial when you're fishing small flies on or near the surface.

A lesson I learned when I was guiding was how quickly even experienced fly fishers react when they see trout feeding on top. Most wanted to get a fly tied on and get casting—right now! That doesn't always pay when it comes to small flies. Taking those few extra minutes to carefully observe what the trout are doing and what's going on in the environment around them will pay off when you make your first cast.

The first thing to do when you see trout rising is to make the initial observations as detailed in chapter 3. Look for adult insects in the air and on the water. Note if more than one species of insect is hatching. It is critically important to determine if the trout are taking on the surface or just under the surface. Note if the trout are feeding sporadically or with a regular rhythm. Study the riseforms.

The final observation to make is whether the trout are feeding singularly, in pods, or in feeding lanes. If the trout is a single, is it rising steadily? If the fish are in a pod, are any of them rising with a particularly predictable rhythm? Are those fish positioned downstream or toward the outside of the pod? If the fish are rising in a feeding lane, are there any especially steady risers? You should also note currents between you and the rising fish that might impact your presentation.

THE LAST-MINUTE CHECK FOR FISHING SMALL DRY FLIES AND EMERGERS

Once you've made your observations, use them to determine any last-minute modifications you will need to make to your equipment before you move into your casting position. It's surprising how many times I decide to stretch the leader to make sure it's straight, recheck a knot, or pull fly line off the reel and respool it so that I'm sure it will feed out smoothly when I get a fish on. I want everything to be set because I know that my first cast is often my best shot at hooking a difficult fish rising to small flies.

I place the most emphasis on my terminal tackle during my last-minute check. I use the most flexible, limp 6X tippet material I can find, and I make sure it is a minimum of 20 percent of my leader length. I often extend it to 30 percent of the leader or even a little more, figuring that it might pile up a bit and give me a few more seconds of drag-free drift. I've found that the 6X works fine in most small-fly fishing situations. I

will go to 7X in very still water for very spooky trout or to attain a more natural action when I use a clinch knot on size 24 flies or smaller. The bottom line is I don't believe that the difference in diameter between 6X and 7X bothers trout much. I do think what bothers trout is when the fly doesn't drift naturally because the tippet material is too heavy.

I don't usually use fluorocarbon leaders, but I do occasionally use a fluorocarbon tippet for certain small-fly situations. I often use a dry fly and dropper (also known as a trailer) setup when I find trout porpoising to emergers just under the surface. A small emerger pattern tied with absorbent material, such as rabbit underfur or a tiny 1.5mm beadhead, will sink, but a monofilament tippet, which tends to float, may keep it on the surface. If you use fluorocarbon tippet material, which sinks more readily, between the dry fly and dropper, it will help pull the fly into the strike zone. You can also fish the emerger by itself. Just lightly grease everything except the last 6 to 12 inches of the tippet with a paste floatant. The fly will still sink into the strike zone, and you can watch the greased floating portion to detect strikes.

PRESENTING SMALL FLIES ON OR NEAR THE SURFACE

Fly fishers often misunderstand presentation to simply mean casting, but the implication of the word is considerably broader. Presentation means the approach to the trout, positioning yourself for the most advantageous cast, choosing the right cast to make, executing the cast, mending line if necessary, and hooking the trout when it strikes.

Drag

Drag is best defined as the unnatural movement of a dry fly on the water's surface. The most obvious example is when you cast straight across the stream with no slack in the fly line. When your fly hits the water the current immediately pulls the fly line downstream, forming a belly. That belly in turn drags the dry fly across the water's surface in an unnatural fashion. You'll probably see little V-wakes pushing out from the sides of the fly as it motorboats across the water. As a rule, trout don't appreciate this. The unnatural movement puts them on guard and may actually scare them away or at least put them off the feed for a while. The ideal presentation makes the fly look like you simply dropped it on to the water's surface without a tippet, leader, fly line, or you attached to it. That's the ultimate drag-free drift.

Drag is especially challenging for small-fly fishermen because its effects can be more difficult to detect when fishing a fly that may not even be visible on the water's surface. The best course of action is to assume that drag exists on anything but the shortest of casts and act accordingly. Consider your position before the cast, use casts that put slack in the leader, and if necessary, mend the fly line once it's on the water to counteract drag.

I always seem to be admonishing small-fly fishermen to get as close to the trout as they can, and rising trout are no exception to this most basic rule. If at all possible, always move your feet closer to the fish before you lengthen your cast! Getting close gives you the best chance to control drag and see a small fly on the water's surface. The ability to see a floating fly means that you'll see strikes more clearly. And that greatly increases the chances of getting a solid hookup. Seeing your fly on the water's surface is the most important single thing you can do to improve your small-fly fishing success.

Approach

Of course, there will be plenty of times when the light or some other factor prevents you from seeing your tiny fly and you'll have to go blind, but always at least try to position yourself where you'll be able to see the fly. This means consider-

ing the light when you plan your approach. It's usually better to have the light at your back, but the best way to tell if the light will help you see your fly on the surface is to observe the water from a distance at the same angle you plan to approach and fish it. If you can see naturals on the surface, the odds are good you'll be able to see your artificial, too. Also remember that you only need the light to be right for a few feet where the fly will pass over the trout. You don't have to see the fly perfectly either. A "chromy" patch of water will silhouette the fly nicely, and that's all you need to see a strike.

There are other ways to fine-tune your approach. Wear neutral-colored clothing. Remember the old guide's saying that friends don't let friends wear neon colors on the river. When conducting the approach, use streamside vegetation or banks to break up your silhouette. Lower your profile by kneeling when necessary. If possible, find a casting position on the bank. When you do get into the water, practice slow, no-wake wading. As you get closer to the trout, lower your profile by getting into a crouching tiger position. The crouch doesn't make you invisible, but it does make your shape less threatening to the trout. It may sound corny, but I watch herons for lessons on approach.

At one time the only recommended approach to a trout feeding on the surface was from downstream. The idea was that trout feed with their noses into the current, thus an approach from downstream was least likely to be detected. In addition, it was thought that a straight upstream or upstream-and-across cast was less likely to fall prey to drag. Today small-fly fishers find themselves approaching feeding trout from upstream, too. When you do, remember that the trout are facing in your direction. Odds are you will not be able to approach as closely as you would from downstream without spooking the fish. It's even more crucial to break up your silhouette, lower your profile, and wear neutral-

Best Casting Positions for Most Surface and Near-Surface Small-Fly Feeding Situations

UPSTREAM AND ACROSS
Advantages:
• It is a fly-first presentation.
• You get longer drag-free drifts.

Disadvantages:
• There is a higher possibility of spooking trout on approach.
• There are possible drag-producing current conflicts.

DOWNSTREAM AND SLIGHTLY ACROSS
Advantages:
• You can make a curve cast to avoid putting leader over trout.
• The approach is less likely to spook trout.

Disadvantages:
• The conflicting current has a slightly higher chance of producing drag.

STRAIGHT DOWNSTREAM
Advantages:
• The approach is less likely to spook trout.
• Fewer conflicting currents means less drag.
• You can use the riseform disruption of downstream fish to hide the leader when fishing to trout farther upstream.

Disadvantages: The leader passes over top of trout.

colored clothing when executing an approach from upstream.

Casting Position

The primary goal of the approach is to get as close to the rising trout as possible without spooking it. How close you get will depend on whether the water is flat or riffly, its clarity, and the direction of your approach. Getting close will allow you to make a more accurate cast and better control drag on the fly. Figure that the less line you have on the water, the less drag on the fly.

Always consider what's between the trout and you. Are there conflicting currents that will make a drag-free drift difficult or impossible? Is there overhanging brush? Are there obstructions behind you that could prevent a backcast?

My two favorite casting positions to trout feeding on small flies on or near the surface are downstream and slightly across from the fish or upstream and across from the fish. A downstream-and-slightly-across position lessens the chance of spooking fish during the approach and reduces the chance of microdrag during the drift. Although the upstream-and-across casting position does increase the chance of spooking the trout, it allows you to make a fly-first presentation where the trout sees the fly before the tippet. If neither of these casting positions is available, I look for a straight downstream or an across-stream position. I use an upstream position when a fly-first presentation to a difficult trout is crucial or when other casting positions that are less likely to spook the trout are impractical.

Casts

Casting is at the heart of presenting small flies to rising trout. Unlike the arrow-straight casting pond casts you see on TV, most fishing fly casts were developed to introduce slack into the leader, which facilitates a drag-free drift of the fly. The crucial slack isn't always pretty—it may be in the form of a series of S curves or simply a pile of leader on the water's surface—but it gives the fly a few more precious moments to float in a natural fashion before the current attacks the leader and line. And it's surprising how attractive a well-executed slack-line cast begins to look when you know it's the answer to fooling a trout into taking your dry fly.

Subtle Microdrag

current

Even in slower-moving water where little surface disruption is observed, a change in the streambed topographically may create microcross-currents, upwelling, downwelling, and even upstream currents that can create drag on the fly.

To make an S-curve or wiggle cast, wiggle the rod tip back and forth parallel to the water's surface at the completion of the forward cast. The wiggle will create a series of S curves on the water's surface.

Before you learn any slack-line casts, remember that all effective casts begin with proper positioning on the stream before the cast is executed. Also, leader design can facilitate slack-line objectives. Make sure your tippet is at least 2 feet long. Adding even more length to the tippet will often cause it to form a few S curves of slack on the water's surface. A soft monofilament tippet and midsection will create more slack than one constructed with hard monofilament. Experiment with tippet length until you find a length that produces S curves. If it piles up, it's too long. If it stays straight, it's too short. Also, consider fine-tuning it even more with a George Harvey-style leader design.

Upstream Cast. Most dry-fly fishers learn the upstream cast first. It's the cast that's probably the least affected by drag. I consider it a foundation cast for small-fly work. The cast can be useful in its purest form and also in conjunction with slack-line casts, curve casts, or as an upstream-and-across cast. In its most basic form, the upstream cast is made from a position directly downstream from the feeding trout. The fly is cast 2 or 3 feet upstream of the rising fish in such a way as to allow only the leader to pass into the trout's field of vision. If the fly is cast too far upstream, the fly line itself may pass over and spook the fish.

The most common mistake beginning fly fishers make when executing the upstream cast is to allow too much slack line to accumulate on the water's surface as the fly drifts downstream toward them. It is crucial that this slack be retrieved by stripping it from behind the forefinger of the rod hand. Managing slack line is important when executing the upstream cast because if too much slack is allowed on the water's surface, it becomes impossible to set the hook when a trout takes the fly.

The key to the check or bounce cast is to end with the rod tip in a close-to-vertical position.

There are some useful small-fly refinements that you can make to the basic upstream cast. Don't position yourself directly downstream from the rising trout. This is especially true for slow-moving water where a wary trout sipping small flies will detect the tippet on anything but a perfect cast. If you can cast slightly across and upstream to the trout, there is less chance that the tippet section will be detected. It will also be easier to manage slack line on the water's surface as the fly drifts downstream.

Incorporate one of the slack-line casts described below into your upstream or slightly across-and-upstream cast. Although it may seem like a cast presented directly upstream would float drag-free downstream, that is not the case. Although the current is going generally downstream in the river, there are microcurrents going upstream, cross stream, downstream, or swirling up toward the surface or down toward the bottom. All of these adverse currents can create drag on the dry fly. Adding more slack to your cast increases the odds that you can overcome their effect.

Executing a slack-line cast can look pretty intimidating, depending on what source you read or which casting guru you talk to. One book I read named fourteen different slack-line casts. It doesn't have to be that hard. If the frustratingly wide loop that many beginners cast is stopped a bit high on the forward cast, it results in a glorious pile of slack on the water's surface. The problem is that most beginning casters are trying to tighten their loops up and straighten their lines out rather than make great slack-line casts!

The trick is to be able to create slack in the line and leader when you want it. The key to understanding slack is to understand that the fly line and leader will do what the tip of the fly rod does.

S-Curve or Wiggle Cast. If you complete a forward cast and then wiggle the rod tip back and forth parallel to the water's surface just as the line straightens, it will produce a series of S curves when it lands on the water. The S-curve

PARACHUTE OR PUDDLE CAST

The parachute cast is accomplished by keeping the rod high on the forward stroke.

Gently lower the rod tip toward the water just as the loop unfurls at the end of the stroke. The fly line will land first as the leader collapses.

cast is a great way to add a little slack to an up-stream or across-and-upstream presentation. Use the S-curve cast when you present the fly down-stream, and it will unfold like an accordion, all the while providing a drag-free drift. Some fly fishers prefer to wiggle the rod back and forth perpendicular to the water's surface, which also creates nice piles of slack line. Try the cast both ways to decide which works for you.

Check or Bounce Cast. Make this slack-line cast by abruptly stopping or checking the rod during the forward stroke, which causes the leader and line to bounce back toward the caster in a series of S curves. Start by false-casting 10 to 15 feet more line into the air than you need to hit your target. Overpower the delivery stroke slightly and stop the rod between 11 and 12 o'clock. When the loop straightens, bounce the rod back toward you with a slight jerk. End the cast with the rod tip close to vertical. The result will be a series of S curves on the water's surface. It's a good cast for adding slack to upstream or downstream casts in riffles or broken water. In addition, the check cast can be effectively exe-cuted in breezy to moderately windy conditions.

Puddle or Parachute Cast. The puddle or parachute cast creates slack by dropping the rod tip toward the water at the end of the forward stroke. This releases energy from the loop and the fly line floats gently to the water's surface fol-lowed by the leader, which forms a puddle of S curves on the water. Vince Marinaro describes it as a soft cast very much like a false cast with the "punch shot eliminated." To make the cast, keep the rod tip high on the forward stroke. Marinaro recommends that, as the fly line is unrolling on the delivery stroke and the fly is about over the connection between the leader and fly line, gen-tly lower the rod tip toward the water's surface. The leader will then collapse into a puddle of loose coils on the water. Over the years, the pud-dle cast has become one of my favorite small-fly slack-line casts because it's more accurate than

When the leader lands on the water, it will form a series of S curves.

A wiggle cast is an effective way to introduce slack into a downstream cast.

other slack-line casts. The one drawback is that it's difficult to execute in windy conditions.

By modifying and combining aspects of the S-curve, check, and puddle casts, most drag-producing situations can be overcome.

The refinement of slack-line casts has increased the popularity of downstream casts for fishing small flies. Small-fly fishers have found that very selective trout on hard-fished waters often refuse the fly when the leader is cast over them. The downstream cast allows the angler to present the fly to the fish first. The S-curve, check, and puddle casts all lend themselves to downstream presentations where neutralizing drag is crucial to success. Remember that extra stealth is required when approaching feeding trout from upstream and that longer casts and longer leaders may be required.

An effective downstream cast will land the fly 3 to 10 feet upstream of the feeding fish with enough slack in the line and leader to deliver the fly drag-free to the trout. If the fish does not take the fly, allow it to drift 3 or more feet downstream from the trout. At that time, flip the rod over to one side so that the fly line can be picked up off the water away from the trout.

Very long downstream drifts to hyperselective trout were pioneered on smooth-flowing small-fly waters such as the Henry's Fork and Delaware River. Anglers there make presentations well above the feeding trout and then feed line out in loose curves as the fly drifts toward the fish. Some downstream line-feed presentations may actually employ the entire length of the fly line.

Reach Cast. I believe that the reach cast, also known as an aerial mend, and its variations are the most important specialty casts for small-fly fishers to know. It allows the caster to mend line upstream in the air when casting directly across stream, across and upstream, or across and downstream. It's the most effective way to get long drag-free drifts on smooth water types such as glides. The reach cast is made by casting di-

THE REACH CAST

The reach cast lands on the water with the fly line at an angle upstream from the fly. It's accomplished by aiming the fly where you want it to go, but just as the line straightens on the delivery stroke, move or reach the rod in an upstream direction.

As the fly drifts downstream, follow it with the rod tip.

Continue to follow the fly as it drifts downstream. Extend your arm to extend the drag-free drift.

Upstream, Upstream-and-Across, and Across-Stream Presentations

APPROACH AND POSITION
- Don't wade unless necessary. If you wade, enter the water quietly and practice wakeless wading. Disturb the water as little as possible.
- Lower your profile: kneel on the streambank, and when wading, crouch.
- Use shoreline vegetation or streambank cuts to break up your profile.
- If possible, position yourself in shade. If not, have the sun at your back unless it casts your shadow over the fish.

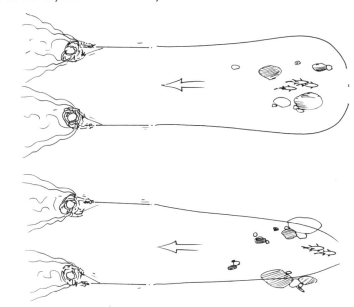

UPSTREAM PRESENTATION (PREFERRED)
- Position yourself not quite directly downstream of the rising trout.
- Avoid casting fly line over the fish. Cast so that only the first half of the leader passes over top of the fish.
- Strip in slack line as the dry fly drifts downstream toward you.
- Use a check cast or parachute cast to create slack in the leader for a drag-free drift.
- Use right-hand or left-hand curve cast on spooky risers to avoid drifting any leader over the trout.

UPSTREAM-AND-ACROSS PRESENTATION
- Position yourself downstream and cast across stream from the trout.
- Try to position yourself close enough to avoid conflicting current speeds that could cause unwanted drag. If that's not possible, hold the rod high to lift as much line off the water as possible, avoiding drag.
- Avoid casting fly line over the fish. Cast no more than the first half of the leader over the fish.
- Use a check cast or parachute cast to create slack in the leader for a drag-free drift.
- For longer drifts, it may be necessary to mend line.
- Manage slack line if necessary.

ACROSS-STREAM PRESENTATION
- Position yourself across the stream from rising trout.
- There is a greater possibility of spooking trout in across-stream position; you may not be able to approach very closely.
- Conflicting current speeds may require you to hold the rod high to get fly line off the water and avoid drag.
- Use a reach cast where possible.
- Very long drifts may require the reach cast and a mend.

Advantage of a Down-and-Across Reach Cast Over Other Down-and-Across Slack-Line Casts When Casting Across Current

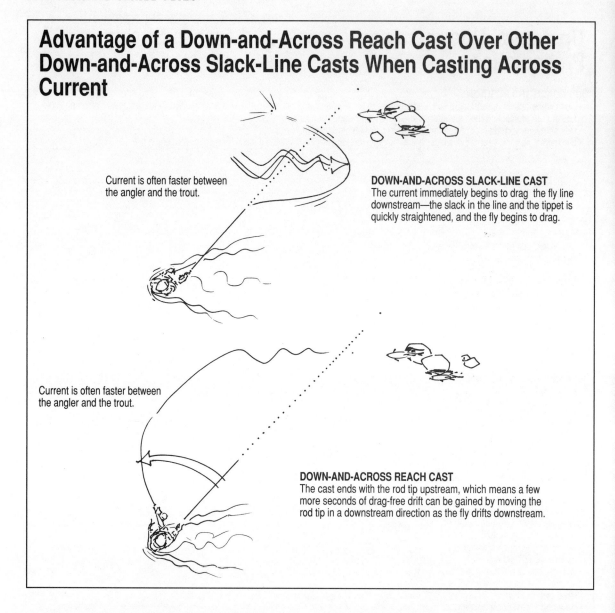

Current is often faster between the angler and the trout.

DOWN-AND-ACROSS SLACK-LINE CAST
The current immediately begins to drag the fly line downstream—the slack in the line and the tippet is quickly straightened, and the fly begins to drag.

Current is often faster between the angler and the trout.

DOWN-AND-ACROSS REACH CAST
The cast ends with the rod tip upstream, which means a few more seconds of drag-free drift can be gained by moving the rod tip in a downstream direction as the fly drifts downstream.

rectly to where you want the fly to land on the water's surface, but just as the line straightens on the delivery stroke, move the rod smoothly in an upstream direction. The fly will land where you aimed it, but the line will land upstream at an angle from the rod tip, allowing the fly to pass over the fish before the leader. As the fly drifts downstream, follow it with the rod tip to extend the drag-free presentation. Under optimal condi-

tions, a well-executed reach cast will often allow a drag-free drift of 15 feet or more.

I find myself using variations of the reach cast all the time when fishing small flies. In more complex conditions where slack in the leader is required, I'll add an S-curve or check cast to the reach cast. The down-and-across reach cast has become my standard cast for many of the small-fly situations where I used to make an upstream or an upstream-and-across cast. It's especially useful for situations where I am casting over a section of faster-moving water and must land the fly on a slower-moving section of water on the other side of it. It's a scenario commonly encountered when you're in an across-stream or midstream position casting to a trout rising along the opposite bank.

To make a down-and-across reach cast, position yourself upstream and across from the rising trout. Aim the cast down and across stream to exactly where you want the fly to land. Right when the fly line straightens out on the delivery stroke, extend and straighten your rod arm while simultaneously moving the rod upstream and parallel to the water. Reach out as far upstream as possible. When the fly lands on the water, immediately follow its drift downstream with the rod tip to put slack in the line and prevent drag.

You probably won't get as long a drift with the down-and-across reach cast as you might with a standard reach cast, but it will allow you to angle the fly line across faster-moving water *and* then provide enough slack by moving the rod tip downstream to give you the 12 inches or so of drag-free drift required to fool a trout.

The beauty of the down-and-across reach cast is that it ends with the rod tip upstream, which means you can capture a few more precious seconds of drag-free drift by moving the rod tip downstream as the fly drifts downstream. An S-curve cast or even a parachute cast ends with the rod tip directed downstream. That makes the fly line on the water's surface vulnerable to drag almost immediately.

Sidearm Casts. In addition to slack-line casts and the reach cast, a well-rounded small-fly fisherman will occasionally need a sidearm cast to get the fly up under streamside branches or, more importantly, when it's necessary to keep the rod and line movement out of a spooky trout's visual field. The sidearm cast is nothing more than a basic fly cast tipped over on its side. The loop unrolls parallel to the water's surface.

SIDEARM CASTS

A sidearm cast may be necessary when presenting a small fly along the bank where there is overhanging vegetation. To make the sidearm cast, simply tip your normal casting stroke over on its side parallel to the water's surface.

An across-the-body sidearm cast may be necessary, depending on which side of the stream you are on. Make the across-the-body sidearm cast by holding the casting arm across the body and tipping the rod over until it's more parallel to the water's surface.

To make the sidearm cast, make the basic casting stroke with the rod parallel to the water's surface. Slack-line casts can be incorporated into the sidearm cast where necessary.

Right- and Left-Hand Curve Casts. The final casts necessary for your small-fly repertoire are the right- and left-hand curve casts. Curves are obviously helpful for getting around mid-stream rocks or boulders, but their real value for fishing small flies is when you are casting upstream to a rising trout but don't want to put your leader over the fish. To make a left-hand curve cast, execute a sidearm cast, but overpower the delivery stroke. The added energy to the fly line will cause it to hook to the left, forming a curve. The more difficult to execute right-hand curve cast begins with a sidearm cast that is underpowered on the delivery stroke. The loop will lack the energy to completely unfurl, forming a right-hand curve on the water.

The ability to execute a predictable curve cast is among the more challenging tasks that small-fly fishers are called upon to do, but it is also a cast that can save the day on particularly hard-to-catch trout. It's one of those casts that I find myself practicing in the middle of the day when things are slow and I'm waiting for the evening hatch. Remember that different methods work for different casters. You may find that it helps to make a snappy turn of the wrist right when you're executing the power stroke. Or maybe you'll have to shock the rod a bit on a sidearm cast. The only way to find out is to practice. You'll be glad you did when you find yourself in a situation where a curve cast is the only answer.

Mends. I prefer to deal with drag by my choice of casting position and/or the type of cast executed, but as much as I try to avoid it, I find that it's sometimes necessary to deal with it after the cast has been made and the fly line and leader are on the water. A typical situation is an across-stream cast where the current catches the fly line, creating a downstream belly, which produces drag on the fly. This situation can be remedied by an upstream mend.

To mend line, lower the rod tip and flick a loop of line upstream with a rolling motion of the wrist. The tip of the rod will form a crisp upside down U shape. The result will be an upstream, drag-resistant belly of line rather than a

RIGHT-HAND AND LEFT-HAND CURVE CASTS

Make the right-hand curve by underpowering the delivery stroke of a sidearm cast. In this case, it's an across-the-body sidearm cast being underpowered.

Make the left-hand curve by overpowering the delivery stroke of a sidearm cast.

Although a curve cast can be used to deliver a fly around rocks, it may be more valuable in small-fly fishing situations when you want to make a fly-first upstream or slightly across-and-upstream presentation.

MENDING LINE

When a downstream belly forms in the fly line, it is necessary to make a mend before it causes the fly to drag.

Roll the rod over in the form of an upside-down U to flip a loop of line upstream.

The resulting upstream belly will prevent drag.

downstream, drag-creating belly. Overpowering the mending flick will sometimes cause the unwanted effect of lifting the fly off the water and away from feeding trout. With practice, mends can be made so that the fly moves very little from its position on the water.

Sometimes an eddy or backwash creates a drag-producing upstream belly in the fly line. Use a downstream mend of the fly line to correct it.

Presentation

Good presentation is the sum total of understanding drag, making a successful approach, selecting the best casting position, choosing the right cast, and properly executing that cast. The best presentation has one additional ingredient—the insight and intuition that a fly fisher has developed in similar situations over the years. Maybe there's a little drag-producing back eddy that is best countered with a downstream-and-across reach cast rather than a downstream parachute cast. It could be there is a breeze that must be countered with an across-the-body cast. Perhaps a sidearm cast is necessary to avoid spooking the trout.

Ultimately, every presentation is a product of all the other presentations that you've attempted under similar circumstances. For today's presentation, you apply the discoveries you made yesterday that worked and discard the techniques you tried that didn't work. You experiment with new ideas and combinations of techniques to solve old and new problems. It's what good fly fishing is all about.

Good presentation takes practice and experimentation. You have to develop a patient approach to a judicious casting position. Ultimately, the basic casts should be instinctive. These skills are your tool box. When you become proficient with the tools, there are an infinite number of ways to use them to solve small-fly fishing situations.

It will take *conscious* practice. When you've caught a trout or two using one combination of

Downstream and Downstream-and-Across Presentations

APPROACH AND POSITION

- Trout are more likely to spot you when you approach from upstream. You might not be able to get as close as you could with a downstream approach.
- Take special care with the approach. Use streamside vegetation and streambank cuts to break your profile.
- Wade out into the stream as little as necessary to position yourself for the downstream cast. Practice wakeless wading; disturb the water as little as possible.

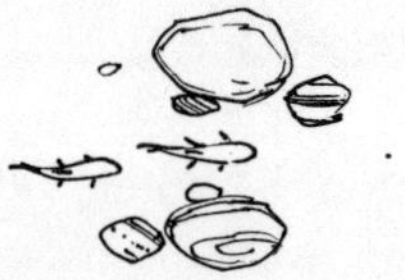

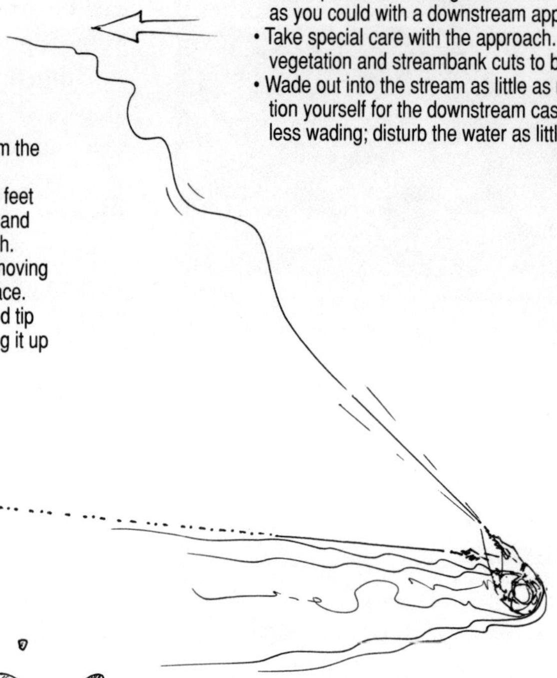

DOWNSTREAM PRESENTATION

- Position yourself not quite directly upstream from the rising trout.
- Use the S-curve cast. The fly should land 2 to 5 feet upstream of the trout. The curves in the fly line and leader should allow it to drift drag-free to the fish.
- If you need additional slack, wiggle out line by moving the rod side to side, parallel to the water's surface.
- To avoid spooking the fish, move the line and rod tip to one side or the other of the fish before picking it up for a recast.

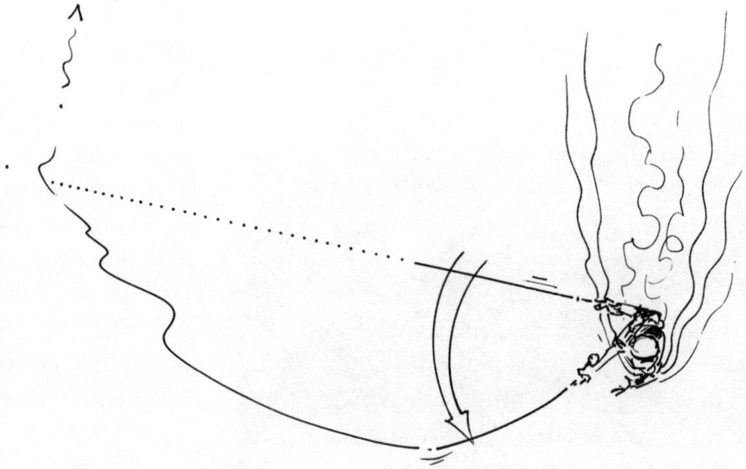

DOWNSTREAM-AND-ACROSS PRESENTATION (PREFERRED)

- Position yourself upstream and across from the rising trout.
- Use a reach cast. Aim a false cast downstream to the point where you want the fly to land. At the end of the presentation stroke, move the rod sharply upstream. The fly will land where you aimed downstream of the fly line. Follow the fly with the rod tip as it drifts downstream.
- For more slack, try the reach cast with an S-curve cast applied at the end.
- Conflicting current speeds may require you to mend line or hold the rod high to get the fly line off the water and avoid drag.

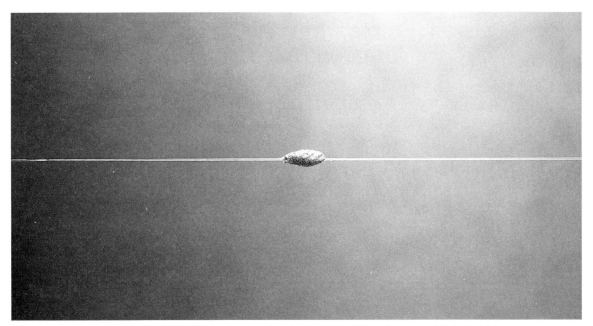

A tiny bit of strike putty rubbed onto a leader knot makes it easier to detect strikes when a small fly isn't visible.

techniques, try something new just to see if it works. Maybe you'll find out that under those conditions you can hook a spooky riser when you present the fly upstream to the fish, but no matter how far you position yourself upstream of the fish, a downstream presentation just doesn't work because the trout spots you. Then on another day you attempt a downstream presentation but decide to crouch down to change the appearance of your silhouette, and the trout takes the fly! Maybe on the next outing you discover that by moving upstream a step or two all the problems you were having with drag disappear into thin air.

The trick is to keep learning. Don't let yourself believe that a certain presentation always works in a certain situation. Keep experimenting. Keep trying new combinations. It *will* get complicated, but ultimately you'll internalize the mechanics. And then it will begin to feel like there is less and less between you and the trout. That's the way you want it.

ADDITIONAL CONSIDERATIONS
Seeing the Fly
The most common concern novice small-fly fishers voice is that they can't see their fly on the water's surface. Actually, all of us, no matter how much experience we have fishing small flies, would prefer to be able to see them. With practice you will get better at using the available light and your casting position to help you see the fly, but sooner or later you'll have to come to terms with fishing a fly on the surface that you can't see. You'll be doing better than most if you can spot a size 20 or smaller fly on the surface 50 percent of the time.

There are some standard tricks that small-fly fishers use to help them see tiny flies. Try greasing the tippet and leader 12 to 18 inches behind the fly. You'll be able to see the floating section of leader, which can then be used as a strike indicator or at least to indicate the vicinity of the fly's location. Sometimes a tiny piece of the sticky-back disposable-foam type indicator, a smidgen

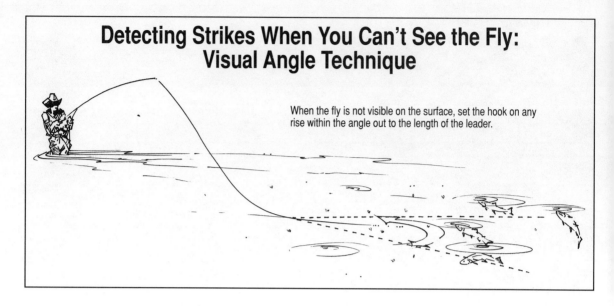

Detecting Strikes When You Can't See the Fly: Visual Angle Technique

When the fly is not visible on the surface, set the hook on any rise within the angle out to the length of the leader.

of strike indicator putty rubbed on a knot, or a small but visible dry fly placed 12 to 18 inches from the fly is the *only* way to detect a strike. From an aesthetics point of view I'll always opt for a single fly first, then a small dry fly used as an indicator, and finally the little strike indicator. I sometimes get some ribbing for it, but I'm one of those small-fly fishermen who is concerned with aesthetics when I fish tiny flies on top. I want the experience to be as pure as possible with as little as possible between me and the trout. But you do have to be practical, too. . . .

Eventually, you'll find yourself in the situation where the trout are so spooky that they won't allow you to use any kind of dry fly or floating strike indicator. It happens often when I fish the Frying Pan River with my friends John Gierach, A. K. Best, and Mike Clark. All of these guys are very good small-fly fishermen, and I asked them once how they detected strikes to a small fly when they couldn't see it. There were a few moments of silence before John said, "the Force."

John has a way of making the truth humorous. Sometimes all you have to go on is instinct. And good instinct comes from practice. You just

have to fish the fly blind and set the hook whenever you think that the rise you see is a trout taking your fly. It's hard at first, but just like the subtle nymphing skills, if you put the time in, you will develop skills that are crucial if you want to fish small flies at the highest level possible.

It's not just hocus-pocus either. There are ways to develop and improve your instinct. Use the visual angle technique to determine where on the water's surface your fly is most likely to be. When the fly line drops to the water, imagine an angle of 20 or 30 degrees on either side of it that extends out for a foot or two beyond the length of the leader. It's a good bet that your fly will be within that arc. Watch the area in the arc, and set the hook if anything rises in it. A consistent casting style using the same length leader all the time will aid you in fine-tuning your sense of where the fly is. Some fishermen use the same idea but prefer to consider the area around the fly within the radius of their leader length. You have to watch more area, but if there aren't too many rising fish, it can be quite effective, too.

Also be on the lookout for any rise near your fly that doesn't quite look like the other rises

Detecting Strikes When You Can't See the Fly: Radius Technique

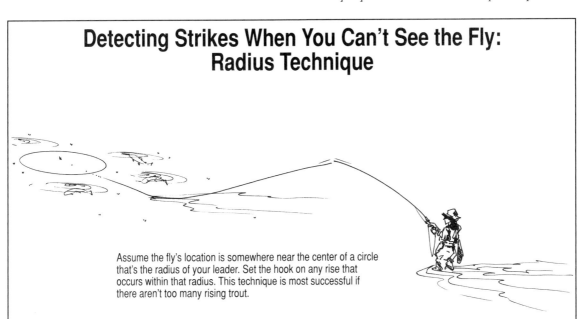

Assume the fly's location is somewhere near the center of a circle that's the radius of your leader. Set the hook on any rise that occurs within that radius. This technique is most successful if there aren't too many rising trout.

around it. Trout will sometimes take an artificial fly in a slightly different way than a natural. Some small-fly fishermen take that to mean that they haven't quite matched the natural or there is a glitch in their drift, but what the heck? Take a strike however you get it. You can expect to see this odd type of rise on a pretty regular basis, too.

Fishing small flies on or near the surface presents unique problems. What the insects lack in size they usually make up for in numbers. Hatches and spinner falls may produce astronomical numbers of naturals on the water. The huge number of insects makes it worth even a larger trout's time to eat such tiny bugs. But the availability of so many naturals impacts fly fishers in several ways.

At the height of heavy small-fly hatches and spinner falls, trout often develop a clearly defined feeding rhythm. The textbook advice for dealing with this has always been to simply time your cast to coincide with the trout's feeding rhythm. That's easy to say, but it's not so easy to execute. What it means on a practical level is that you are

going to have to make a *lot* of casts. Figure some of your casts will be out of sync with the rising fish and some will be off target. Some will be on the mark, but the fish will choose to take a natural instead of your artificial. The more on-target casts you make, the better your chances. That's another reason to get as close as you can—it's easier to be accurate. In addition, resist the tendency to flock shoot at pods of sipping or porpoising trout. Flock shooting seldom works. Pick one steadily rising fish to work to.

Small-fly enthusiasts disagree over how close to put the fly to a rising fish. If I'm positioned downstream and slightly across from a steady riser in slow water, I try to put the fly within a foot of the trout. But if I'm executing a reach cast from an upstream-and-across position, I may lead the trout by up to 2 or 3 feet. I might drift a straight downstream cast 10 or 15 feet to a rising trout.

The key is to weigh the trade-offs. The closer you can put the fly to the trout, the better your chances of coinciding with its feeding rhythm—

The Grass Cast

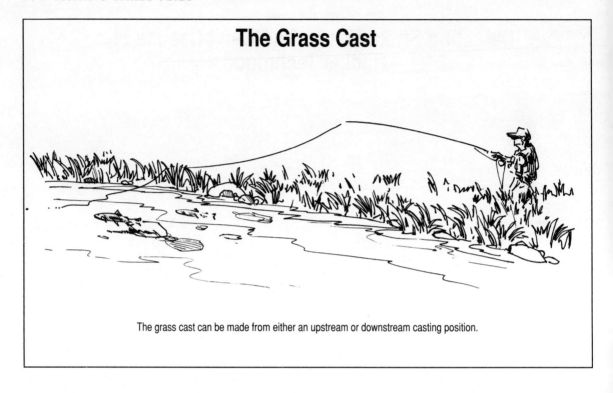

The grass cast can be made from either an upstream or downstream casting position.

and the greater the risk of putting the fish down. If you allow the fly a longer drift, you probably won't put the fish down, but the chance of drag increases.

Special tactics may be required for especially spooky trout or where it is very difficult to get a drag-free drift. When casting to a trout rising close to the bank on your side of the river, consider the grass cast. Stand well back from the fish and make a cast so that the fly line and even a bit of the butt section of the leader land on the streamside grass or gravel and only the finer part of the leader and tippet land on the water. Needless to say, this cast is fraught with danger—a twig or rock that snags the line might prevent you from hooking the fish, but if it's your only shot, what do you have to lose?

Sometimes a fish will be rising right up against a boulder in a way that makes it impossible to get a drag-free drift to the fish. In this situation try bouncing the fly off the rock. It will often hit the rock and drop straight down into the trout's feeding lie with enough slack in the tippet for a drag-free drift. For trout rising close up against the opposite bank, lightly cast the fly onto the bank upstream from the fish and then gently pull it into the water.

Steady risers in very smooth water may spook when the fly line is cast over them either because they see the movement of the line in the air or because of water droplets coming off the line and disturbing the surface. You may have to false-cast at an angle that's outside the trout's vision and then lower the rod close to the water on the presentation cast to make the loop less visible to the trout. If a steady riser is spooking to your tippet, consider timing your presentation to use the disturbance caused by its riseforms to hide the tippet.

A drag-free presentation is usually the most effective way to fish a small fly on or near the surface. However, there are times when action applied to the fly on a tight line is effective. Leonard Wright popularized the sudden inch for fishing larger dry-fly patterns. The sudden inch is accomplished by suddenly skating the fly an inch or two upstream on a tight line. The added action is sometimes what it takes to induce a trout to strike. At times I've found the tactic to be effective during microcaddis hatches or when the wind is blowing hatching mayflies across the surface. On windy days when midges are hatching, a Fore-and-Aft imitation tied to an extra long tippet can be wind-dapped on the surface by holding the line off the water downwind and then lowering the tip to dap the fly near a rising trout.

Fishing small flies on the top and in the surface film is tricky business. The best small-fly anglers have mastered special casts that help them make drag-free presentations. Those casts must be coupled with on-the-water flexibility and creativity. Don't fall into the trap of letting a small-fly fishing situation lull you into a sense of false security because you have observed a similar situation in the past. Take a few minutes to observe a rising trout and make sure there are no new variables. And then apply your knowledge from past experiences to the problem.

CHAPTER SIX

The Fine Arts of Striking, Hooking, Playing, and Landing Trout on Small Flies

It's the early season and I'm poking around on the South Platte River. Even though the fishing is pretty good this time of year, I sometimes like to take an hour or so to just walk the river. It gives me a chance to see if trout are holding in any new areas, and I like watching other people fly-fish. I've learned a lot over the years by just watching other fishermen. I have also seen drama unfold in front of my eyes. Today is one of those days.

There is a novice dead-drift nympher on the river. I can tell he's new to the technique by the amount of time he's taking with each presentation. I can also tell he's had instruction. He water-loads and nicely casts the rig across and upstream. When the line lands on the water, he immediately mends it. Most self-taught nymphers learn about mending as soon as the fly hits the water later on in their development. A guide will teach it from the git-go. As the strike indicator drifts downstream he holds his rod high and follows it with the rod tip. His line management is particularly good. There are no coils of line laying on the water, but rather he holds a small loop of line under the index finger of his rod hand. That's another sign that he's had some instruction. That little loop of line will be released to act as a shock absorber when he hooks

up and the trout takes off with his size 20 nymph imitation that's attached to the fragile 6X tippet.

He really is doing everything right. I watch a couple more casts and drifts. On the next one I notice the strike indicator tweak just a bit. It's almost imperceptible. It's probably just the weight nicking the stream bottom, but a more experienced nympher would have investigated it by setting the hook. A few casts later he does pick up on a more obvious strike and sets up hard. The tiny imitation is immediately popped off and all of the electricity goes out of the line. I watch his shoulders slump just a bit. He retrieves his rig, assesses the damage, adds some tippet material, replaces the lost fly, and goes back to fishing.

I know he'll get more strikes because the blue-winged olive nymphs are especially active now. It's actually a very good time to learn the ins and outs of nymphing because you get a lot of strikes. And lots of strikes mean lots of chances to fine-tune your technique.

Before I head upstream, he pops off two more flies by striking too hard and loses one trout that he manages to hook but breaks off when he plays it too aggressively. I leave because I figure he doesn't need me watching him retie the fly for the fifth time. It's a classic example of the small-fly school of hard knocks. At least he's getting some shots. By the end of the day he'll have figured out just how little it takes to firmly stick a tiny fly into a trout's mouth, and with luck he'll be on his way to learning just how much pressure he can exert on a small fly and light tippet when he's playing a trout. He's doing the research right now. Time on the water is the only sure way I know to develop the small-fly touch. And make no mistake, hooking, playing, and landing a trout on a small fly is the most delicate dance a fly fisher will ever be invited to.

Over the years I have learned that the most difficult aspect to teach beginning small-fly fishers is how to detect a strike, actually striking, and then playing the trout on light terminal tackle. Ultimately, skill in these fine arts of small-fly angling will come with time and perseverance on the river, but there are some things you can do to speed up and fine-tune the process.

DETECTING STRIKES

The basics of detecting a strike on or near the surface were covered in chapter 5. If you can see the fly, a strike will be more obvious. If you can't see it, techniques such as narrowing down the water surface area where you expect the strike to occur and watching for unusual riseforms or underwater flashes are helpful. At first you need to set the hook whenever you have any physical indication of a strike or just a sense of the strike. It's very difficult to teach what a sense or an instinct for a strike is. The best way to understand it is to realize that there is a lot of information about what's going on on the water's surface coming into your mind through your eyes and hands. Sometimes that information may be converted directly to action, that is, you set the hook before you have time to consciously think about it.

An athlete would say it's an eye-hand coordination thing. Maybe you sense just a tiny change of color on the surface because a trout has turned or maybe the fly line feels a little different

in your hand and, bam, you strike. Sure, some of the time it's going to be a false alarm, but you'll be surprised how often it's a trout. The very best small-fly fishers I know not only realize that this kind of sixth sense exists, but they consciously try to develop it.

Stories about the difficulties of detecting strikes when nymphing with small flies, especially for beginners, are legion. Aside from the basics of strike detection detailed in chapter 4, the best advice I can give (and it's often not what a novice small-fly nympher wants to hear) is stick with it. You will need time to develop a sense for the difference between the nymph imitation catching the bottom for a moment and a trout taking the fly. Stick to short-line nymphing until you have a sense of these differences. Practice watching the strike indicator *and* the water where you suspect the trout are at the same time. Sometimes there will be a subtle change in the water's color, or even the surface when the trout turns to take the fly. At the beginning, set the hook every time you have the slightest sense that you may have a strike. This is how you fine-tune your instinct. Eventually you'll have a conscious and a subconscious catalog of what constitutes a strike as opposed to a snag.

Finally, when you begin landing a few trout, pay attention to where you hooked them. If you find that the fish was actually hooked on the outside of the mouth or the gill cover, there is a good chance you were late on the strike. The trout probably took the fly and then rejected it, but the fly was still close enough to the fish to hook it near the mouth when you set up. The slightly late strike is often the result of poor mending practices. Nymphers sometimes inadvertently allow the strike indicator to drag slightly downstream of where the flies are. This makes it more difficult to detect a strike. Also, using a little too much weight or just simple inattention can result in a late strike. With more experience, these outside-the-mouth hookups

Detecting Strikes When Dead-Drift Nymphing

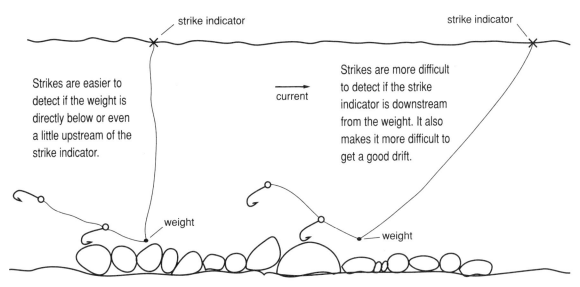

strike indicator

strike indicator

Strikes are easier to detect if the weight is directly below or even a little upstream of the strike indicator.

current

Strikes are more difficult to detect if the strike indicator is downstream from the weight. It also makes it more difficult to get a good drift.

weight

weight

Keep the strike indicator over the weight by mending the fly line whenever necessary.

will decrease. Trout hooked in the tail or toward the rear are most often simply foul-hooked.

STRIKING

The two most common ways that trout are lost when striking with a small fly are improperly timed strikes and overzealous strikes.

The timing of the strike is dependent on casting position and, to a lesser degree, the trout's riseform. A straight upstream or across-and-upstream presentation gives you a mechanical advantage because when you strike you're pulling the hook into the fish's mouth. From a practical aspect it means that you can set the hook just about as soon as you see the trout's head come up and take the fly. If you find that you're missing strikes or pulling the hook out, odds are you're setting up just a hair early. Try waiting until you see the trout begin to go down with the fly and then set. It's a difference of little more than a microsecond, but fishing small flies often comes down to splitting hairs.

A downstream cast puts you at a mechanical disadvantage because you're pulling the hook *away* from the fish's jaws. If you set the hook the moment you see the trout rise, the odds are that the strike will be missed because the trout won't have time to close its mouth over the fly. It's best to wait until the fly disappears into the trout's mouth and then pull the trigger. Although, once again, the time between seeing the trout's head appear and the fly disappearing into its mouth takes only microseconds, it can seem a lot longer. Buck fever is a real possibility here. All I can say is try to hang on.

As a rule, expect most of the feeding activity during a hatch of small flies to occur in slower water. Once in a while a microcaddisfly hatch will break the rule, but that's about it. The dynamics of many spring creeks and tailwaters that are host to heavy small-fly hatches are such that the trout can find slower water that delivers a steady stream of emerging insects to them. It

Striking from Upstream or Downstream

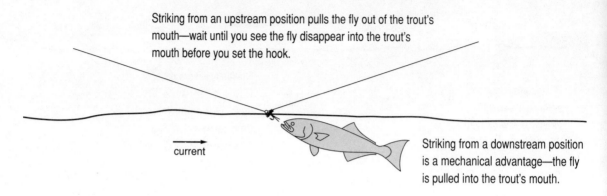

Striking from an upstream position pulls the fly out of the trout's mouth—wait until you see the fly disappear into the trout's mouth before you set the hook.

current

Striking from a downstream position is a mechanical advantage—the fly is pulled into the trout's mouth.

makes the metabolic equation work in their favor—they can eat more of the smaller insects and expend less energy doing it.

Slower water usually means slower rises. A slow rise makes it easy to overreact and set the hook too soon. It's crucial to wait until you see the trout's head come out of the water or even until you see the fly disappear into its mouth. Expect to see Marinaro's compound and complex rising behavior when the trout drift downstream with the fly to scrutinize it before they strike. You must hold back and wait for the actual take before setting the hook!

Pay special attention to head-to-tail rises, when the trout's head is actually coming out of the water, and head rises. You should wait to strike until you see the trout begin to descend with the fly.

Although the delicate tippets that small-fly fishers use today are three or four times stronger than the ones I used when I was just learning to fish small flies, more trout are still lost to overzealous striking than for any other reason. Surprisingly, the tippet itself doesn't break that often, but rather the knot at the fly or a knot farther up the leader. A tiny hook will often bend before the tippet or a knot fails.

With practice, most small-fly anglers develop a sense of what their terminal tackle can handle,

but there are some techniques that can help bridge the gap until you develop that sense. Always check to be sure that your tippet is long enough. A longer tippet will give you an extra edge because it stretches more.

Most fish caught on flies are hooked with an anchor-point strike or a strip strike. In an anchor-point strike the fly line is held against the cork of the rod handle by a rod hand finger, or it's held tightly in the line hand. The strike is made by moving the rod either sharply up or to one side. This drives the hook into the fish's mouth. The line alone is used to set the hook in the strip strike. Typically, the rod is pointed toward the water as the fly is being retrieved. When a strike is detected the line hand sharply pulls the fly line to set the hook. A combination of a strip strike and the rod motion of an anchor strike makes for an even more forceful strike.

Executing a strike with a small fly is almost the opposite of an anchor-point or strip strike. The wire on a small hook is so small that it takes virtually no force to drive it into a trout's mouth, so the idea is to *lessen* the force of the strike. Some anglers simply release their line anchor point and set the hook with a short upward strike. The small amount of unanchored slack line between the line hand and the stripping guide acts as a cushion. The downside of the

A soft strike can be accomplished by forming a circle with the index finger and thumb of the line hand and simply allowing the fly line to slide through the circle during the strike.

practice is that line control may be lost until the fly line can be placed back under the anchor finger.

An alternative that utilizes more slack line is to form a circle with the index finger and thumb of the line hand and simply allow the fly line to slide through the circle during the strike. Once the trout is hooked, the line is grasped by the line hand and then transferred to the anchor under the index finger of the rod hand until excess line is spooled on to the reel.

It's also possible to set a small hook with a mini-strip strike by gently tugging the fly line and not lifting the rod at all, but it takes practice to resist lifting the rod tip. The advantage of the tug is that the fly stays in the water. If you miss the strike, the trout may follow the fly and strike again. In the end, anglers who fish small flies on a regular basis find that they will learn to modify their normal striking technique to a flick of the wrist or a dampened lift of the rod tip to accommodate small flies and delicate tippets.

Dead-drift nymphing with small flies requires some different striking rules. The take on a dead-drifted nymph can be difficult to detect. At first you will simply have to set the hook whenever you think you have a strike. Later on, you should experiment with techniques that allow you to set the hook if you have a strike, but don't remove the fly from the water if it's a false alarm.

If I think I have a strike I like to gently lift the fly to feel for weight. If a trout is on, I'll feel its weight and the electricity of something that's alive on the other end of the line. Since I've already removed the slack from the system by lifting the rod, all I have to do to hook the fish is make a short, gentle, but sharp set. Sometimes the fish will turn and hook itself when it feels the light pressure! If I don't detect a fish when I lift the rod, I lower the tip, which allows the nymph to continue its drift. That way, the fly stays in the water where it still has a chance to entice a trout to strike. It's crucial to remember to gently set the hook if you detect a trout when using the feeling-for-weight technique. You will lose the trout if you get excited when you feel it but fail to set the hook.

When you are sight-fishing to nymphing trout with dead-drift techniques, make a point to watch the strike indicator *and* the trout itself. If the fish opens its mouth, tilts from side to side, or moves slightly out of the feeding lane, set the hook with either a lift or horizontal side strike. If you are able to watch your nymph imitation drifting toward the trout, see it disappear into the fish's mouth before you strike. You may just see a wink of white as the fish opens and closes its mouth.

PLAYING THE TROUT

Trout hooked on or near the surface can be expected to make one or more runs. The first run has the most potential for disaster because the trout is still strong and effective line management can be difficult. The most important thing to do when you've hooked a large trout on a small fly is to allow and facilitate its first run. All your emphasis should be placed on preserving the tippet and maintaining a solid hookup. You must allow the fish to smoothly take line out when it's going away from you, but you must retrieve any slack line that might occur if the fish changes direction. The less tension you can have on the line while still managing its smooth withdrawal and resolving any slack-line problems, the better.

The key to accomplishing these sometimes contradictory goals begins with preparation. Prepare for the possibility of a strike before every cast. Don't have any more fly line piled up on the water than is necessary for the cast. Make sure the line doesn't have any tangles or kinks that would prevent it from running smoothly through the rod's line guides. Make sure you aren't standing on the line and it isn't looped around your leg. Set the drag on your reel at the lowest possible setting that will still prevent back spooling.

It's important to maintain the proper amount of tension on the line when playing a trout.

Once the cast is completed and the drift has begun, manage the slack line so that you can effectively strike the fish *and* efficiently feed out line during the initial run. When the fish is hooked and the run begins, hold your hands at shoulder to head level with the rod at about the 11 o'clock position. This holds the fly line off the water, which will reduce drag, and the rod's flexibility will act as a shock absorber for the tippet.

Avoid holding the rod straight overhead with arms fully extended. It may look like the photos in the fly-fishing magazines, but it reduces your options. If your arms aren't fully extended over your head, you'll be able to raise the rod a little higher if an emergency develops and you need to take up some slack. You'll also be able to see

the rod tip, which will help you assess how much pressure you can put on the fish.

If the fly line isn't coming off the spool smoothly or if you think the drag setting is too high, don't hesitate to strip line off the spool with your line hand and control the tension as it runs under the first or second finger of your rod hand, which should be holding the fly line against the cork grip. With any luck the trout will run out all the line that was lying at your feet, and you'll be in the optimal position of being able to play it from the reel.

Unfortunately, the trout won't always run all of the line out and sooner or later you will have to manage slack line while also playing the trout. You'll need a system in which you can maintain contact and control of the trout and safely store

Rod Position for Playing Trout

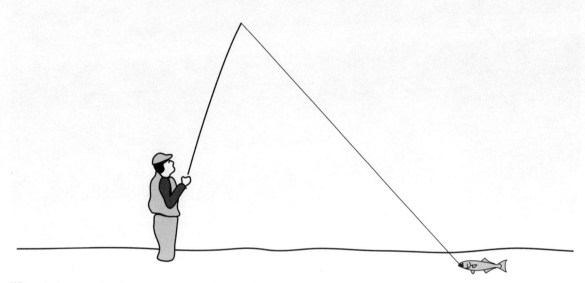

When playing a trout, hold your hands at head level or lower with the rod in the 11 o'clock position—this will allow you to raise the rod over your head if you need to quickly take in slack.

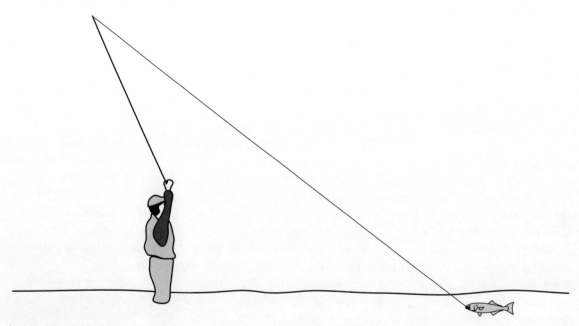

Avoid holding the rod with your arms fully extended over your head when playing a trout. This position won't allow you to raise your arms if you need to take up slack.

Left: The anchor finger allows the angler to maintain proper tension on the trout until there is an opportunity to reel in excess fly line. *Right:* It may be necessary to use the last fingers of the rod hand to evenly distribute fly line back on to the reel when playing a trout. Fly line that isn't evenly distributed on the reel could tangle if the trout makes another run, possibly resulting in a broken tippet.

the slack fly line at your feet until you have the opportunity to reel it in. In most situations you can manage the slack by retrieving the fly line under the first or second finger of the rod hand and then holding it against the cork. This anchor finger on the line keeps you in contact with the fish when you're retrieving line. It allows you to maintain the proper amount of tension on the trout while storing the slack line at your feet until you have the opportunity to reel it in and play the trout off the reel.

It's important to wait until the trout calms down before you attempt to get the excess line back on the reel. If the fish is still feisty, just manage the slack by retrieving line under your finger. When the trout makes short runs, let the line run out from under your finger. Eventually the trout will want to hold and rest. I usually consider this the end of the first run and take the opportunity to reel the excess line back on to the spool. You may need to use the little finger or the last two fingers of your rod hand to evenly distribute the fly line back on to the reel when retrieving slack line. Fly line that is hastily reeled on to the spool in a haphazard fashion may tangle if the trout makes another run, which could result in the tippet breaking.

It's important to remain constantly vigilant for any changes in the trout's behavior when reeling in the excess fly line. If the trout makes another run, be prepared to feed line out under your finger. If it races toward you, be ready to strip line in under your finger, and if that isn't fast enough, you'll have to raise the rod higher or where possible take a few steps backward to maintain the tension.

The exceptions to maintaining steady tension on the trout are if it jumps, violently shakes its head, or snags up in weeds or on the bottom. A jumping trout hooked on a small fly is always dangerous. If it jumps and shakes its head, the fly may be thrown. If it jumps on a taut line, it could break the leader. There isn't a lot you can do to prevent it from throwing the fly, but you can drop the rod tip a bit to give it some slack, which may prevent it from breaking the tippet. The same holds true for a fish that is boring down and shaking its head. Better to drop the rod and give it a bit of slack than risk breaking the leader.

Large spring creek trout are notorious for heading into the weeds when hooked. The best approach is to make every attempt at preventing them from getting into the weeds in the first place, but if they go in anyway and you can't wade close enough to noodle them out by reeling the rod tip right up to their nose and gently pulling from an upstream position, try lightening up on the line tension. Sometimes when the tension is reduced the trout will back out into the open water where it can be played. You can also try the opposite—keep the tension on the trout and hope it tires enough to back out or allows you to pull it out of the vegetation. Either strategy is worth a shot because they are about the only options you have.

When playing a trout on light terminal tackle, try to keep it upstream or across stream from you. This is the most positive angle to drive the hook deeper into its jaw, and the fish will be fighting the current and you, which means it will wear out more quickly. The hard and fast rule of playing a fish is that the less time you play it, the less there is that can go wrong. If the trout does run downstream, get out of the water and follow it on the bank until you once again get it positioned across or upstream from you. As you quickly move downstream along the bank to the fish, reel the line in and hold as much of it as possible off the water to decrease drag. If the better part of the fly line is on the water, there is more than enough drag to break a delicate leader or pop the fly out of anything but the most securely hooked trout.

The trout may make several more runs where you'll want to carefully manage the line, but the first run is typically the strongest and most unpredictable. Every trout plays differently, but a common quirk I've found with larger trout in heavily fished tailwaters or spring creeks is that they'll simply drop down to the bottom in a holding position when hooked rather than make an explosive first run. This is particularly true for fish hooked by dead-drift nymphing tactics.

It's an interesting situation because you have a large trout hooked on a tiny fly attached to a delicate tippet that hasn't expended *any* energy. You'll never land it if you stand there all day just maintaining the tension on the line, but you'll break it off if you try to horse it in. In addition, the trout could decide to burst into its initial run at any moment. My experience has been that if the trout is going to bolt into an initial run, it will happen fairly soon if you keep the tension on it. Sometimes you can induce a run by turning the trout's head.

Do this by holding the rod low to the water on one side of your body and pull smoothly and steadily just enough to turn the trout's head

Playing Trout on Small Flies

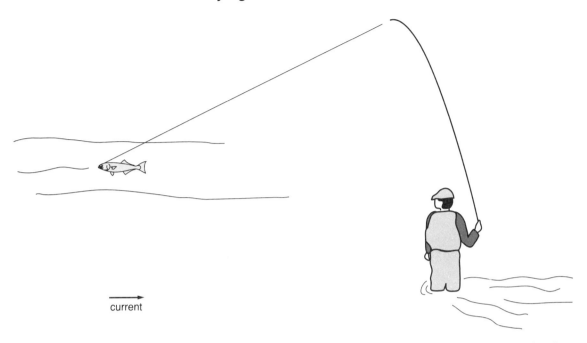

current

Play the trout upstream or across stream from you. It's easier to hold line off the water, which reduces drag on the fly. It's also easier to control the fish when it isn't swimming with the current.

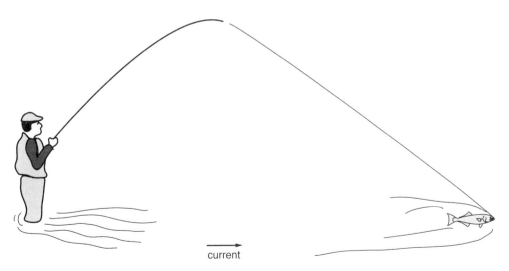

current

Playing a fish downstream from you means you're also playing the current. The trout has the advantage when it runs downstream because more fly line ends up on the water, which creates more drag on delicate tippets and small hooks. When the trout gets downstream of you, get up on the bank and follow it. Reel line in until you get the trout across or upstream from you.

Turning a Trout's Head

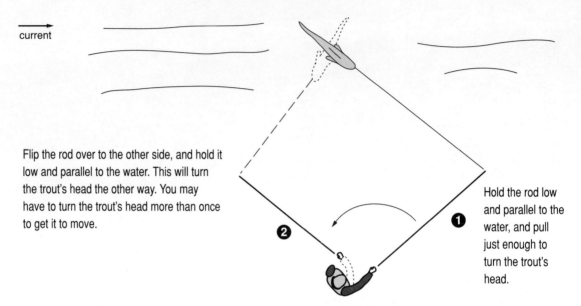

current

Flip the rod over to the other side, and hold it low and parallel to the water. This will turn the trout's head the other way. You may have to turn the trout's head more than once to get it to move.

Hold the rod low and parallel to the water, and pull just enough to turn the trout's head.

Turning the trout's head will often induce a holding or resting trout that is hooked to make a run, which will wear it out, allowing the angler to bring it to net more quickly.

a little bit. If nothing happens, flip the rod over your head to the other side of your body and do the same thing. The movement will turn the fish's head one way and then the other, which is usually enough to induce it into a run. This is an extremely delicate operation. You want just enough pressure to turn the head, and it must be applied smoothly to prevent stressing the leader and hook.

If the head turning doesn't work, try wading closer to the fish. It will probably kick out into a run when you get too close. Once again, be ready to feed out line and facilitate the run.

LANDING THE TROUT
Eventually, the trout will wear down, and it will be time to land it. Once again you enter dangerous territory. If you choose to use a landing net, hold the rod at arm's length away from your body and angled slightly over your head and then quietly place the net in the water. It's easiest

to gently guide the trout head first into the net. Another option for deeper water is to place the net directly downstream from the trout and then lower the rod tip a bit, allowing the fish to drift tail first into the net. Try to keep your movements as smooth and unthreatening as possible. Be prepared for the possibility that the trout will make another run. The strength of that run may be quite surprising.

If the fish is near the net and gets rowdy, it's best to not start stabbing the net in the water in an attempt to land the fish. If you inadvertently hit the fish with the side of the net, it's quite possible that you'll knock the tiny hook out of its mouth or get it snagged in the net, where the trout will break it off.

You might also consider beaching very large trout if your net isn't large enough. You'll probably have to play the fish out a bit more, which I don't like to do, but it's the price you pay for

The easiest way to land a trout is to guide it head first into the net.

attempting to drag them out of the water. They don't like that at all.

A hemostat-type pliers is useful for removing small hooks from the trout. If the fish is still feisty when you're trying to remove the hook, it may help to turn it upside down, which seems to calm the fish. Be sure to watch the trout when you release it after the upside down maneuver because sometimes it disorients them a bit and you may have to right the fish.

Lately, I've been using a small-size Ketchum release tool, which lets me release the trout without ever taking it out of the water. The tool slips around the leader, and you run it down to the fly, which you can pop out with a turn of the wrist. It works much better if you use barbless flies, which most small-fly fishers do as a rule anyway. I think I may have to play the trout a little longer before I can release it with the tool, but from a conservation point of view, I think I mitigate that because I never have to touch the fish.

PLAYING TIME

The surest sign of an accomplished small-fly fisher is that he lands trout quickly and efficiently. Bringing a trout to net as quickly as possible is good for the angler because the less time the trout is played the less there is that can go wrong. And it is good for the trout. Any fish that's going to be released should be stressed as little as possible.

Every small-fly fisher goes through a stage when he plays trout much longer than necessary. It only makes sense that you'll err conservatively when playing a larger than average fish on a size 22 fly attached to a 6X tippet! It takes time to figure out the limits of such delicate terminal tackle. But it's important to strive to find those limits.

Remember that 6X tippet now rates out at about 3-pound test and 7X tippet is 2½-pound test. That's much better than the ½-pound test I remember when I first started fishing small flies. It's amazingly strong stuff. If you keep your tip-

pets long, work to turn the trout's head this way and that, which will wear it out more quickly, and keep the trout upstream or across stream from you, you'll be surprised how quickly you can land it.

RELEASING TROUT

Fly fishermen release trout for a lot of reasons. If you plan to release trout caught on small flies, land them as quickly as possible *and* be sure they are revived when you let them go. The best way to do this is to gently hold the trout in slower-moving water with its head into the current. Cradle it under the belly while holding it at the wrist of the tail and then gently swish it back and forth. You'll see its gill covers start working and pretty soon it will have enough energy to swim out from your hands. Observe the trout as it swims away to make sure it doesn't go belly up. If it does, retrieve it and revive it again.

Needless to say, it's best to not remove a trout from the water if you plan to release it. If you must lift the trout out of the water, wet your hands first and limit the fish's time out of the water to a minimum. For photographs, have someone hold the trout underwater, head into the current, while the camera is set up and focused. When everything is all set, lift the fish up out of the water, release the shutter, and immediately get the fish back in the water.

One of the things I like most about fishing small flies is that the challenge doesn't end when I've hooked a trout on a tiny imitation. It is always in doubt whether I'll get the fish close enough to see what it looks like. I know I'll need all my skill and finesse if I want to have a look. Some fly fishers are content to know that they have fooled the trout into taking a small fly. They don't care if they lose it after the strike. I'm not that way. I still haven't gotten over how gorgeous a rainbow trout or a brown trout or a brookie or a cutthroat trout is. I still have to see them. . . .

To release a trout gently, hold the trout in slower-moving water with its head into the current.

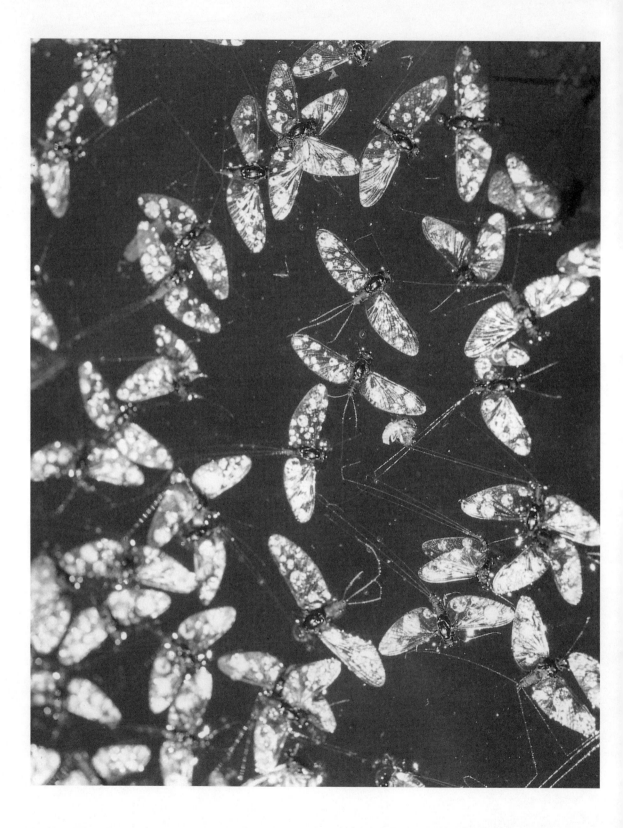

CHAPTER SEVEN

Fishing the Major Small-Fly Hatches

The South Platte River in Cheesman Canyon was Colorado's first designated catch-and-release area, but the water was renowned among fly fishers well before those special regulations were implemented. The canyon has always been known for its large and fiendishly difficult-to-catch rainbow and brown trout. The special regs water comprises the first three miles of river below the Cheesman Dam—so it's a classic bottom-release tailwater. Those large trout got large by eating a diet of foods that are mostly the size of a size 18 hook or smaller. The fact that thousands of fly fishers show them tens of thousands of fly patterns every year contributes to their selectivity.

It all combines to make the canyon a necessary course in any small-fly fisher's postgraduate curriculum. Fly patterns have been developed exclusively to fool Cheesman trout. Stealth small-fly dead-drift nymphing tactics have been employed by canyon anglers for years. In the early 1960s Charlie Jenkins developed a matchless bamboo rod taper with Cheesman Canyon trout in mind. And the largest fish get more elusive every season.

It's the Saturday after Thanksgiving 2003, and I'm walking the Gill Trail into the Canyon. It's a brilliant, warm, bluebird day with all the implications that a day like this has. It's warm because a high-pressure system is pushing air down the eastern slope of Colorado's mountains. The trade-off for the shirt-sleeve weather is that Chinook winds might blow me off the river. The best strategy is to get on the water early when I might get a few hours of relative calm before the wind comes up.

As soon as the canyon comes into view, I head down a side trail to the first section of water above a fence that crosses the river at the boundary of the exclusive Wigwam Club. There is a long, flat pool there with only the whisper of a few small riffles. I head for a picnic table that's set back along the bank under a ponderosa pine. The table is a good place to watch the water while I rig up. Despite the fact that the parking lot was crowded with the cars of holiday weekend anglers, the only person I can see is fishing the heavy riffle at the head of the pool.

I've learned to come to this flat water when the river is crowded because most fishermen aren't up to the frustrations of trying to catch these trout. There's virtually no riffles to cover presentation errors. Thick aquatic vegetation in the main channel makes landing any trout you might hook difficult. In addition, there is very little shoreline vegetation to cover your approach, which means that the trout have seen plenty of fly fishermen move into casting position. Actually, they've seen so many that they seldom break their feeding rhythm when they see another one. But you can rest assured they are on guard. Refusals to perfect presentations are not uncommon.

The trout are already working near the surface. From my shaded observation post at the picnic table I can see bulging riseforms along with an occasional simple rise to the surface. It's easy to see the trout pick off their prey under the surface and then return to their feeding lie. Any surface rises are clearly being made to a midge that pops into the air without spending much time on the surface. Without disturbing the water with my seine, I figure that the bulging riseform are to the midge pupa associated with the adult.

I rig up with a favorite soft-hackle midge imitation because I'm seeing more bulges than sips and experience has taught me that I'm more likely to score here on a midge pupa imitation presented in the film than an adult imitation on top. I switch over to a long fluorocarbon 6X tippet and tie the fly on with a clinch knot. I've had my eye on several fish rising near the bank on my side of the river. There is an almost imperceptible current line that they are holding in. One of them is feeding regularly on pupae just below the surface.

My approach is simple. I crouch down and quietly move out as far as I can and still stay in the shadow of the picnic table pine. My plan is to cast downstream and across to the fish. My fly line will land completely on the gravelly streambank. Only the leader, tippet, and fly will land on the water. I wet the partridge aftershaft feather of the soft-hackle fly with salvia because I've found that it doesn't dry out as fast when I false-cast it. I want the fly to sink a bit when it lands on the surface and this will help.

I then quickly focus and concentrate on the exact spot 1 foot upstream of the rising trout where I want the fly to land, make a few backcasts, and then manage to put the fly very close to that spot. I can see the trout react as the fly makes the short drift toward him. He calmly fins up to meet the fly. He comes closer and closer and closer. And then at the last minute he turns away. It's the prettiest refusal I've ever seen.

I let the fly drift safely downstream of the trout before I lift it off the water. I don't fool around with a second cast before I change the fly. That kind of refusal rise almost always means the gig is up and the only option I have is to try another fly. I unsuccessfully play cat and mouse with the trout for another thirty minutes before I seek out another riser. The results are the same. I'm not discouraged because my very best presentations are often refused here. The upside is that I am alone. I have the trout to myself.

A little later my concentration is deflected by a more energetic rise. I spot a gray speck on the water near it and then another speck pops up in front of my eyes! There is no doubt that blue-winged olives are hatching at the end of November! The trout eagerly take both the duns. For a moment I consider fishing an emerger, which is probably the best choice at this stage of the hatch, but I choose to put a parachute dun imitation on because I want to try to take the risers on a dry fly.

It's my choice and I ply the fish with several imitations, get some refusals, and then decide to go to a floating nymph, which is met with a few more refusals. Before I get crazy switching flies I tell myself I'll change to a snowshoe hare emerger and leave it on no matter what. If I get refusals I'll make sure I'm getting a drag-free drift by changing my casting position or my cast. I return to concentrating on making the best presentations I can. Two hours later I'm still fishing the same pattern when the wind blows me off the river. I've missed three strikes, which I partially credit to the fact that I'm using a different fly rod today. It's much faster than my usual rod. Although I'm setting up on the strikes the same way I always do, it seems like the rod is responding quicker. I need to hesitate just a hair longer . . . or maybe I'm just making excuses and could fix everything by just watching the fly disappear into the trout's mouth before I set up.

I've also picked a few other trout where I felt the hook just begin to grab into the trout's mouth and then pop out. As I head upriver to catch the trail back out to the truck, I pass a slew of anglers fishing the riffles and rocks. A couple of them are bringing trout to the net. I'm happy for them and a bit envious. But I fished my way today. It was on the edge. I used everything I know about fishing small flies. Time didn't exist. I was right there for every moment. It couldn't have been a better day. . . .

That day on the South Platte River had all the elements that I look for when I fish small flies. I had to apply all my small-fly angling skills to a constantly changing progression of insect hatches and the trout's response to them. No matter how much you know about small-fly patterns and small-fly tactics, small-fly fishing success will always depend on how that knowledge is applied to the situation at hand. And that situation, in one way or another, will always come down to the nuances of feeding trout.

At the beginning, it will be enough to identify that the trout are keyed on blue-winged olives or microcaddis or midges. You'll catch some fish with just that, but if you're observant you'll begin to realize that there are some segments of a hatch where you are significantly more successful than others. Then you'll begin to refine your tactics. You'll realize that a hatch is a progression of events and that you must match your fly imitation to where it fits into that progression.

Ultimately, you'll observe that the hatches of the various small-fly species progress in different ways. The cadence of the Trico hatch is different from that of the pale morning dun even though they're both mayflies. A midge hatch will have some twists that never occur when mayflies

hatch, and microcaddis are a world apart from anything else. You'll pick up other details such as matching specific riseforms to specific times during a hatch. And then you'll find you can match the hatch, but you can also match the *riseform*. If you've put the time into developing your basic small-fly fishing skills, an understanding of these nuances will give you an angling edge. And that edge will, over time, develop into instinct.

THE ANATOMY OF HATCHES

Hatches of small aquatic insects have certain general characteristics in common. These hatches are often diagrammed in a simplified version as a cycle that begins with the egg. Mayflies and stoneflies have an incomplete metamorphosis. The egg develops into a subsurface-dwelling nymph, which in the case of mayflies ascends to the water's surface at maturity, sheds its nymphal shuck, and enters an air-breathing adult stage. The newly hatched mayfly adults are known as duns (subimago) when they first hatch and then spinners (imago) after molting. Duns have translucent wings and spinners have clear wings. As a rule, stonefly nymphs crawl out of the water, where they emerge as adults and mate. Mayfly and stonefly females then lay eggs in the water, after which they often die and fall spent on the water's surface to complete the cycle.

Caddisflies and midges have a complete metamorphosis. The egg develops first into a larva and then a pupa in the subsurface phase. At maturity the pupae emerge into air-breathing adults, they mate, and the female then lays eggs in the water. In the case of caddisflies and some midge species, the females and males also die after mating or egg-laying and may fall spent to the water's surface.

The important information to understand about small aquatic insect life cycles is:

1. One or two insects don't hatch at a time. They all hatch en masse and the mating takes

place en masse. All the insects hatching at once ensure that some will escape the hungry trout and all the other dangers they encounter on their way to being adults.

2. There are hot-spots in the life cycle when the insects are especially vulnerable to the trout. These occur when they are ascending to the surface, when the adults are emerging from the nymphal or pupal shuck, and when the adults fall spent to the surface after laying eggs.

3. Different species of aquatic insects are vulnerable for different lengths of time during their life cycles.

4. Generally, the trout concentrate their feeding on the most abundant life phase. This means that the trout are more likely to be feeding on ascending nymphs at the beginning of the hatch when they are more plentiful, then on the less plentiful duns that are just beginning to appear on the surface. As the hatch progresses, the trout will switch their attention to the duns as they become more plentiful.

5. The exception to #4 occurs if there is a more vulnerable life phase available—even if it's less plentiful. An example is blue-winged olive duns at the beginning of the hatch whose wings are trapped in the surface film when a strong wind blows them over. They are easy pickings that the trout cannot ignore. Environmental factors such as wind or precipitation will often alter the hatch in some way that increases vulnerability. A less common cause is a genetic glitch that may produce a higher than usual number of crippled or stillborn duns or adults. Occasionally, trout may break their feeding rhythm on plentiful emergers to take the vulnerable or helpless insect as it drifts by simply because the opportunity presents itself.

6. The trout begin subsurface feeding on nymphs or pupae long before the first adult appears on the surface. This is the real beginning of the hatch. Look for the trout to begin heading to the feeding lanes hours before the first adult appears.

Thoughtful small-fly fishermen also consider the times when there's no hatch at all occurring on prime small-fly waters such as spring creeks or tailwaters. Maybe it's just an off day when an expected hatch doesn't occur, or it could be months after a specific hatch is typically encountered. At these times it pays to remember that spring creeks and tailwaters don't have the broad diversity of insect species that a freestone stream does, but the species that they do have, which are usually small in size, are prolific. That means that the trout are probably accustomed to seeing lots of blue-winged olives, midges, pale morning duns, or other small aquatic insect species. You may be able to trigger a strike to a blue-winged olive nymph imitation in July, even though there hasn't been a major hatch since May, because the naturals are still present and numerous in the water and their swimming activity makes them available. Some common small mayfly species and midges are multibrooded, too, which increases the odds that the trout see them throughout the season.

The tactical implications of this are that you should always carry imitations of the major small-fly hatches of the water you're fishing—even if the hatch is not currently underway.

FISHING THE SMALL-FLY HATCHES

Most of the small-fly hatches that I have an intimate knowledge of occur in the Rocky Mountain region. Over the years I've made a point to take notes on the quirky things about our common small-fly hatches that make each one unique. The notes are just simple details most of the time. An example is that during the front end of a springtime blue-winged olive hatch, the trout that are showing a head-to-tail riseform are more likely to be taking emergers a few inches under the surface than a nymph emerging from its shuck in the surface film. But the details pile up. Sometimes they compel me to change my tactics. In other cases they help me identify a feeding behavior sooner, which gives me more time to fine-tune my thinking for that day's fishing. Most importantly the observations have increased my base of knowledge.

I think that a broader base of knowledge increases my small-fly fishing success across the board. That success is mostly the science-based success that is the key to solving fishing problems. But I also think that those fine-tuned observations I've accumulated over the years mean that the hunches I sometimes get when I'm fishing the most difficult, on-the-edge small-fly situations are more often right now than they were ten or twenty years ago.

I've compiled here some of what I've noted about these small-fly hatches over the years. I've detailed the various phases of important hatches and suggested options for fishing to trout that are feeding then. Where it applies, I've also tried to demonstrate how seemingly disparate tactics and observations can be coupled together to increase their effectiveness. Perhaps it might be more important to match the *riseform* at the front end of a midge hatch than it is to match the natural, or maybe you should match a certain cast to a riseform to be most effective in another situation.

Most of what I have to say about the mayflies will concern what I call the big, little three—blue-winged olives, Tricos, and pale morning duns. These are the defining species for our Rocky Mountain waters. I wouldn't presume that all the tactics and observations I present will apply to, say, Pennsylvania or New York, but I have found that much of what I've learned about pale morning duns also applies to the sulfurs found in the eastern United States. The same is true for a Rocky Mountain blue-winged olive and the eastern small blue-winged olives and, to a somewhat lesser degree, Tricos. If my observations and tactics don't exactly fit your particular small-fly fishing situation, I am hopeful that you can use the reasoning that led me to them and, with a little modification, produce a tactic that will provide successful results.

SMALL-FLY PATTERN-TYPE DICTIONARY

It's useful when discussing small-fly fishing tactics to group fly patterns into larger categories, rather than refer to specific fly patterns. The small-fly life cycle diagrams that I presented in chapter 7 use fly-pattern categories such as dry fly, soft hackle, standard mayfly nymph, or larva rather than list numerous specific small-fly patterns. The idea is that there is a group of small-fly patterns that fly fishers can match to specific observations. A head-to-tail riseform at the front end of a mayfly hatch tells me that a floating nymph imitation is in order. The specifics of the pattern will change, depending on the mayfly species that is hatching, but the pattern type won't. A headless head-to-tail riseform during the same hatch indicates that I may need a pattern type that sinks an inch or two below the surface. Good choices would be a tiny soft hackle or maybe a standard mayfly nymph tied on a heavy wire or a beadhead rendition.

I've compiled a dictionary of small-fly pattern types below. A pattern-type group, such as dry fly, is accompanied by photographs of some representative fly-pattern types from that group. Where applicable I've made comments about specific characteristics of some of the fly patterns. My dictionary isn't comprehensive. More than anything, its purpose is to demonstrate that fly fishers don't always have to think in terms of a specific fly pattern as a silver bullet that will solve a specific small-fly fishing situation.

In many cases, success can be achieved by observing where the trout is, what it's doing, how it's doing it, and then matching a fly pattern and fly presentation to that behavior. You may even find that a pattern type generally associated with a specific aquatic insect will cross over to imitate another species if it's of a similar size and fished under similar conditions. I've had suspender-style flies that were designed to match midges work quite well during mayfly hatches when the trout were executing head-to-tail rises.

It's worthwhile to consider that the feeding-activity zone indicated on the hatch charts (e.g., 0.5 inch to surface; 0.5 to 6.0 inches below the surface) may in some cases be as important as an exact match of what is hatching. When trout are feeding heavily at a certain depth, it's sometimes possible to fool them into taking a more general attractor pattern as long as it's close to the same size of the natural and it's accurately presented in the zone where that feeding activity is taking place.

Traditional-style dry-fly hackles have limited use for small flies. Use them mainly in areas with faster water.

Downwing dry-fly patterns are highly versatile. Downwings can represent an emerging mayfly, caddisfly adult, or midge adult. They can also be pulled underwater to represent some species of emerging mayflies.

Parachute-style dry flies are a mainstay with small-fly fishers because the body of the fly rests in the surface film. Always carry parachutes with and without trailing shucks. The major application of the parachute is for mayfly hatches, but it's also useful for midge hatches. Parachutes work with better results in most places that a traditionally hackled dry fly will work.

Palmer-hackle style dry fly. Use a palmer to represent individual midges, with or without a trailing shuck, or in larger sizes to represent midge clusters. It also acts as a mini-attractor pattern during small caddisfly hatches and to a lesser degree mayfly hatches.

Compara-dun style dry flies rank right up with parachute styles because they sit down in the surface film. Carry Compara-duns with and without trailing shucks. The major application of the Compara-dun is for mayfly hatches, but it may also work during midge hatches.

Fore-and-Aft dry fly. Similar to palmer-hackle dry fly. Use as a general small-fly attractor. Good surface action on windy days. May represent knotted midges or an active adult mayfly or caddisfly on the surface.

EMERGERS, CRIPPLES, STILLBORNS ON THE SURFACE OR IN THE SURFACE FILM

Quigley-style cripple. The Quigley imitates mayfly cripples. In smaller sizes it also imitates emerging midge adults.

Suspender-style emergers. Suspenders were designed to float vertical in surface film to represent a midge pupa. They actually work when they're floating vertical or even just lying flat on a side in surface film. A suspender also represents small mayfly duns or emergers.

Stuck-in-the-Shuck midge. This style of fly imitates midges that get stuck in their shucks upon emergence. It will also sometimes work during the front end of a mayfly hatch.

Devil Bug. This fly represents small emerging caddisfly adults when fished on the surface or pulled under the surface. It's occasionally useful during mayfly hatches if the color is right.

NYMPH

Floating nymphs. Use them with or without hackle. Floating nymphs imitate mayfly nymphs in surface film before the dun emerges, or they represent cripples or stillborns. In smaller sizes they are an excellent midge pupa imitation for that moment before the adult emerges.

Standard mayfly nymph. The fly includes tails and a thorax. Always carry some standard mayfly nymphs that incorporate flash. Use them with or without a beadhead. This nymph pattern is a good all-around attractor that can be used before and during small mayfly hatches. It also matches some mayfly nymphs that are a component of behavioral drift.

LARVA

Standard larva. Use the larva to imitate midge and caddisfly larvae. It's a great all-around attractor, especially for midges that are a component of behavioral drift. The fly should have a narrow body that is ribbed to emphasize segmentation. Use with or without beadhead or crystal beadhead.

PUPA

Standard pupa. Use the pupa to imitate midge or caddisfly pupae. The fly should overemphasize the large thorax area. This pattern crosses over to imitate mayfly emergers, too, especially blue-winged olives.

LaFontaine Emergent Sparkle Pupa *(left)* and Deep Sparkle Pupa with bead *(right)*. These patterns are the standard for imitating emerging microcaddisfly pupae. The general flashiness of the pattern makes it a good attractor-style imitation during mayfly and midge emergences, too.

MICRO-SOFT HACKLES

Micro-soft-hackle fly tied with a partridge aftershaft feather. Small soft-hackle patterns deserve a category of their own. They represent nymph and pupa emergers of all small-fly species, adult cripples when fished in the surface film, and drowned spinners. They can be effectively fished using all small-fly tactics at all depth zones. A very versatile small-fly pattern.

Standard small soft hackle tied with partridge feather.

SPENT AND RETURNING ADULTS

Standard spent mayfly spinner. Use this imitation during spinner falls or when duns are trapped in surface film. It sometimes works in smaller sizes during midge hatches. Fish it both on the surface and just below.

SPENT AND RETURNING ADULTS

Drowned spent mayfly spinner. This spinner imitation is designed to sink. Fish it during and after mayfly spinner falls using dry-fly, freestyle-nymphing, and dead-drift nymphing tactics. It's also a good all-around nymphing attractor fly.

LaFontaine Diving Microcaddisfly. This fly represents female microcaddisfly species that dive under the water's surface to lay their eggs. It can also represent an ascending caddis or midge pupa. A diving caddis may also act as an attractor when mayfly nymphs (especially blue-winged olives) ascend to the surface.

TINY MAYFLIES: Blue-Winged Olives

General Information

Nymph: Streamlined body. Two or three tails. Active wiggler/swimmer when collected in seine. Light to moderately dark brown, sometimes with olive highlights.

Dun: Light gray/blue wings, two tails. Light olive to brown/olive body. Lighter color in spring, darker in fall.

Spinner: Brown to dark brown body, dark olive highlights. Two tails. Clear wings. Often appears to be a hook size smaller than the dun.

Size Range: Matches size 18 to 24 hooks.

Representative Genera: *Baetis, Acentrella, Procloeon, Diphetor, Plauditus.*

Hatch Time(s): Typically the first major small mayfly hatch of the spring and the last major small mayfly hatch in the fall, but don't be surprised if you see a dun or two on the water during the summer or winter.

Notes: Many olive species are multibrooded, which means several generations will hatch during the course of the season.

The Real Beginning. I'm constantly amazed at what I call the instance of a blue-winged olive hatch. Maybe I'm wandering around waiting for something to happen and stop to watch a productive-looking trough with a good flow that runs down along the bank. I think I can see maybe one trout in it, but I'm not sure.

Fifteen minutes go by and all of a sudden I see ten trout lined up in the trough. They have literally appeared in the wink of an eye. I wonder how I could have missed seeing them swim into it, but in thirty years of olive hatches I've never seen the trout arrive. They always just appear, calmly finning in the optimal feeding lie. It's like they were beamed down from the mother ship.

Within minutes I'll see one of them take something from the drift, and then another will

SPENT SPINNERS
In some species of blue-winged olives, the females lay eggs in the water and then fall dead (spent) to the surface.
DIAGNOSTIC RISEFORM: Sipping, slow, deliberate simple to complex riseform, bulges.

TACTICS
1. Dry fly.
2. Dry fly with trailer.
FLY PATTERN TYPES
1. Spent spinner.
2. **Drowned spinner.**
3. Soft hackle (imitates drowned spinner).

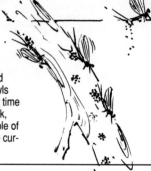

DIVING FEMALES
In other species of blue-winged olives, the female spinner crawls underwater to lay eggs. At that time the female folds her wings back, which often traps a bright bubble of air. Females dislodged into the current are prey for trout.

TACTICS
1. Dead-drift nymphing. Lengthen distance between weight and point fly to add action to the fly. Try lifts and swings.
2. Freestyle nymphing. Use weight on leader or weighted flies. Try lifts, swings.
FLY PATTERN TYPES
1. **Beadhead nymphs—bright bead.**
2. Standard mayfly nymph with flash.
3. Drowned spinner.
4. Soft hackle with flash.

NOTE: Information in boldface type is especially important for this hatch.

Blue-Winged Olive: Match the Life Cycle

FLY PATTERN TYPES
1. Dry fly.
2. Floating nymph.
3. Cripples.
4. Spent spinner—to imitate duns blown over by wind.

Mating swarm.

0.5 inch to surface: Nymphs in surface film emerging from nymphal shuck, drying wings.
DIAGNOSTIC RISEFORM: Sipping, simple to complex riseform, head-to-tail, gulping.

TACTICS
1. Dry fly.
2. **Dry fly with trailer.**
3. Greased leader.

0.5"–surface

Nymphs arrive to just below the surface.
DIAGNOSTIC RISEFORMS: Headless head-to-tail, bulge, wedge.

TACTICS
1. Freestyle nymphing with no weight on leader. Cast unweighted or lightly weighted imitations to riseform.
2. Dry fly with trailer.
3. Strike indicator with imitation.
4. Greased tippet as indicator.
5. Lifts, swings.

Eggs fall, drift to bottom or aquatic vegetation.

FLY PATTERN TYPES
1. Standard nymphs with flash.
2. Soft hackles.
3. **1.5mm or 2mm beadheads.**

0.5–6.0"

Blue-winged olive nymphs continue ascent to surface.

ACTIVE FEEDING INDICATORS
1. Trout suspended higher off streambed.
2. Trout flashing, darting about.

TACTICS
1. Dead-drift nymphing. Lengthen distance between weight on leader and point fly.
2. **Consider swinging fly at end of dead drift or lifting it to imitate actively swimming nymph.**
3. Freestyle nymphing in slower-moving shallow water. Use swings, lifts, and dead drift.
4. Suspension nymphing. Adjust to level where trout are feeding.
FLY PATTERN TYPES
1. Standard mayfly nymphs.
2. **Soft hackles.**
3. Beadheads.

Blue-winged olive nymphs are a component of behavioral drift, which makes them available to trout in varying numbers throughout much of the year.

ACTIVE FEEDING INDICATORS
1. Trout suspended in current near streambed.
2. Trout flashing, darting about.

Blue-winged olive nymphs are streamlined, active swimmers that ascend to the surface during the hatch.

TACTICS
1. **Dead-drift nymphing with one- or two-fly rigs. All water types.**
2. Freestyle nymphing. Slower-moving, more shallow water types.
FLY PATTERN TYPES
1. Standard nymph patterns—match size, color.
2. Standard nymph patterns with beadhead.
3. **Standard nymph pattern with flash to imitate gas-filled nymphal shuck.**

do the same, and another. It's a sure sign that the olives are coming. You'll see most of them daintily picking a nymph out of the drift with a turn of the head, but you'll see some acrobatic turns and flashes, too. Blue-winged olive nymphs are good swimmers. The trout actively chase them down. At this stage of the hatch I expect to see the trout holding anywhere from a few inches off the bottom to about halfway up the water column.

Less observant fishermen often miss this very beginning phase of the olive hatch, and that's a shame because it's nymphing heaven. The trout are lined up and ready to chow down. I'll fish it with a single nymph or soft-hackle imitation placed anywhere from 12 to 18 inches below the weight on a dead-drift nymphing rig. As always, a strike indicator is optional, but don't be worried about it scaring the fish. They'll be pretty busy stuffing themselves this early in the hatch and this far below the surface. They are hungry and feel protected. If you want to stealth things up a little with an expensive fluorocarbon tippet, it won't hurt, but the trout probably won't be bothered by plain old nylon.

This is a great time to practice your freestyle nymphing, too. Cast a weighted or beadhead nymph up and across and watch the trout or where the leader enters the water to detect strikes. Remember to hold the rod high to give the fly a little lift and animation as it drifts downstream. You should try picking a specific trout that's feeding and gently lifting the fly in front of it. Or move a little upstream and across from the fish and make a slack-line presentation or a down-and-across reach cast, which will allow the fly to sink a bit, and swing it in front of the fish. It's one of the few chances you'll get to successfully fish a small fly using close to classic wet-fly tactics.

This preamble to the hatch might last an hour or more. I've seen it go for as long as four hours! If you seine the water, expect to find a wiggling, streamlined nymph with bulging, darkened wing pads. The bulging pads are the evidence that the hatch is imminent.

The Front End of the Hatch. As the emergence progresses, the trout will ascend and hold closer to the surface. At some point their feeding activity will begin to disturb the surface with bulges and, more often, head-to-tail rises. At the very early stages there will be few if any duns on the surface. The trout will probably ignore them unless they're too close-by to resist. The feeding is now centered in the top 6 inches of water. Bulging trout may still attack a nymph or tiny wet fly fished with freestyle nymphing tactics, but if the trout phase into regular head-to-tail rises, figure that any easy fishing you had earlier just went south.

When you first spot the head-to-tail rises, watch them carefully. The odds are that you'll see mostly the top of the back, dorsal fin, and tail. It's uncommon during this stage of the hatch to actually see the whole head or even most of it. The headless head-to-tail rise tells me that the trout are still feeding predominantly on emerging nymphs. This is a good time to rig up a dun imitation and trail a nymph or tiny wet-fly imitation behind it. I usually start with an unweighted nymph. If that doesn't get a response, I go to a tiny beadhead nymph or a standard nymph weighted with just a twist of very light gauge lead wire under the thorax. The best presentation is with a down-and-across reach cast because you can be assured that when you reach the rod upstream it will straighten out the leader. This will present the nymph imitation at the full length of the trailer section between the dun and nymph. That makes it easier to detect strikes and decreases the chance that the two flies will get tangled.

Head-to-tail rising trout during this phase can be very difficult to catch. Some fly fishers are convinced that the trout become superselective to patterns at this stage. And I'll admit to playing the new-fly-every-minute game during

Presenting a Trailer Fly with a Down-and-Across Reach Cast

A down-and-across reach cast swings the rod upstream, which straightens the leader. The trailer fly is presented at the full length of the tippet section between the dry fly and the trailer fly.

An upstream-and-across slack-line cast piles the leader up. The dry fly and trailer fly are then presented much closer together. This may make it more difficult to detect a strike to the trailer fly. It might also make the rig more prone to tangles.

especially frustrating periods. But realistically, I can't see why the ascending naturals would look any different 6 inches from the surface than they do 2 feet from the surface. I now believe there is something different about the way a trout rising head-to-tail takes the natural that is difficult to duplicate with a good fly presentation. I still muddle my way through most of the time, but I now make a point to change my fly less and spend more time experimenting with different casts, lifts, and casting angles.

On Top. The best thing about the headless head-to-tail rise during the blue-winged olive hatch is that it doesn't last too long. The trout usually shift into a classic head-to-tail rise or plain old simple rises as more duns appear on the surface. If you're fishing a dun with a trailer, you'll start to get strikes on the dry fly at this time. As much as you might want to clip off the trailing nymph and just fish the dry fly, I would recommend that you tie a floating nymph pattern on in place of the nymph. This is especially true if you're still seeing the head-to-tail rises. Floating nymph imitations are very effective at this stage of the hatch. The pattern will sometimes outfish a dry-fly imitation for the duration of the hatch on heavily fished tailwaters or spring creeks. The floating nymph imitates that very vulnerable part of the olive's life when the dun is just emerging from the nymphal shuck. Trout will key on the easy pickings.

As more and more duns show up on the surface, your chances of success with a CDC, parachute, thorax, or Compara-dun style dry fly will increase. I do make a point to systematically change dry-fly patterns if I'm not meeting with success, but I try to fish each pattern as thoroughly as I can. Once again, it's just too easy to get into changing a fly every three or four casts if you're not getting strikes, and that's counterproductive. You have to maintain a thoughtful and disciplined attitude as you test the patterns. Carefully watch each drift for refusal rises or any other clues that might indicate interest in the pattern. Sometimes changing your casting position a step or two up-, down-, back-, or across-stream will change the drift enough to elicit a strike. Make every presentation expecting to get a strike.

Over the years I've developed some quirks about the order that I test my dry-fly patterns in. On the rivers where I regularly fish the olive hatch, I've found that I'm more likely to get strikes on a Compara-dun style dry fly when the trout are just beginning to feed regularly on top. Thorax- and parachute-hackle flies seem to do better later in the hatch. I'm not saying that you should adopt this specific ordering for the hatches in your area, but rather be aware of the order in which you test your dry flies. If you notice any patterns developing, experiment with specific orders of presentation the next time you fish the hatch.

If the floating nymph and/or dry-fly imitations aren't productive, you might want to try a little razzle-dazzle. Sometimes the riseform will settle into steady workmanlike simple rises or sips. Although you're seeing rises to the duns on the surface, it may seem like there are just more rises than there are duns. This is a good time to tie on a spent spinner imitation even if you don't find any natural spinners when you seine the water. I can't explain why this tactic works—maybe the trout take the fly for cripples or stillborns or duns that have been blown over and are stuck in the surface film—but it's helped me on numerous occasions. I first tested it when I thought the unhurried sipping riseforms indicated that the trout were taking spent spinners, although when I later seined the water I couldn't find any spinners.

Spinners. Most fly fishers figure the olive hatch is over when the last of the duns are gone. It often is, but sometimes there will be a classic spinner fall later in the day that's worth waiting for. Where I live, a blue-winged olive spinner fall

Blue-winged olive duns that are blown over and trapped in the surface film can be imitated with a spent spinner.

is much more common in the fall. Fishing it can be brutally difficult, but I haven't found anything more effective for it than diligent drag-free presentations. I have found that using a dry fly as a strike indicator is detrimental because the rig often spooks fish that are rising in the thin, clear autumn water. Try a down-and-across slack-line cast or down-and-across reach cast with a single spent spinner imitation. Work on accurate casts and drag-free drifts. It pays to keep the fly on the water as much as possible, too. That means keep the false casts to a minimum.

Oftentimes you won't see a classic spinner fall at all during the olive hatch. That's because the females of some species in the blue-winged olive group actually crawl under the water to lay their eggs. Ernest Schwiebert reports in *Trout* that the females wrap their bodies in their wings and then slip through the surface film to lay their eggs in sheltered places. If you consistently see olive spinners in the air, but then you don't see them spent on the surface, it's a good indication that the females are going under the surface. Careful observation might reveal a flash or trout queued up and feeding. It also indicates that it's time to go back to a tiny wet fly or beadhead nymph to imitate the female's subsurface egg-laying run.

PALE MORNING DUNS

General Information

Nymph: Chunky, rectangular body. Three tails. Fair to moderate swimmer, prefers to crawl along bottom. Light brown to olive brown, sometimes with pale yellow highlights.

Dun: Wings are light gray to pale yellow, often with yellow along leading edge of wing. Body is pale yellow, sometimes with olive tones. Three tails. Duns get smaller as season progresses.

Spinner: Males brown to brown/olive body, sometimes yellow undertones. Females light yellow. Clear wings. Three tails.

Size Range: Matches size 16 to 22 hook.

Representative Genera: *Ephemerella.*

Hatch Time: Predictable hatches June through August and sometimes into September.

Notes: Although this is a western species, my knowledge of the pale morning duns made me feel right at home when I encountered a hatch of sulfurs on New York's Willowemoc River. The dynamics of both hatches had much in common.

The Real Beginning. I used to try to fish the green drake hatch on the Frying Pan River every season. It was always a bit of a crap shoot as to whether they'd be on or not, but I could always depend on the pale morning duns, which hatch at about the same time. They are noted for their predictability. I think that pale morning dun nymphs become active underwater for a shorter length of time before the first duns appear on the surface than do blue-winged olive nymphs. But I also believe that their hatch is so predictable that the trout will often show up in the feeding lanes well before the nymphs do. These early arriving trout are often susceptible to dead-drift nymphing tactics even though prehatch concentrations of the naturals have yet to appear.

Unlike the blue-winged olive nymphs, which are energetic swimmers, the pale morning dun nymphs crawl along the stream bottom rubble.

SPENT SPINNERS
The males fall spent to the surface after mating. Females fall spent to surface after egg-laying.
DIAGNOSTIC RISEFORMS:
Sipping, bulges. Slow deliberate simple to complex rises.

TACTICS
1. Dry fly.
2. Dry fly with trailer.
FLY PATTERN TYPES
1. **Spent spinner.**
2. Drowned spinner.
3. **Soft hackles (drowned spinner).**

FLY PATTERN TYPES
1. Standard nymph with or without flash.
2. Soft hackle.
3. 1.5mm or 2mm beadheads.

Drowned spent spinners.

Note: Information in boldface type is especially important for this hatch.

Pale Morning Dun: Matching the Life Cycle

Mating swarm.

FLY PATTERN TYPES
1. Dry fly.
2. **Floating nymph.**
3. Cripples.
4. Soft hackles.

0.5 inch to surface: Nymphs in surface film. The duns take somewhat longer than other mayfly nymphs to emerge from the shuck.
DIAGNOSTIC RISEFORMS: Simple to complex rises, boils, head-to-tail, even occasional splashy rise.

TACTICS
1. Dry fly.
2. **Dry fly with trailer.**
3. Greased leader.

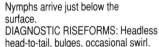

Nymphs arrive just below the surface.
DIAGNOSTIC RISEFORMS: Headless head-to-tail, bulges, occasional swirl.

TACTICS
1. **Freestyle nymphing with no weight on the leader. Cast unweighted or lightly weighted imitations to riseform.**
2. Dry fly with trailer.
3. Strike indicator with nymph emerger.
4. Greased leader as strike indicator.
5. Swings **(pull Elk Hair Caddis under surface and swing)**, lifts.

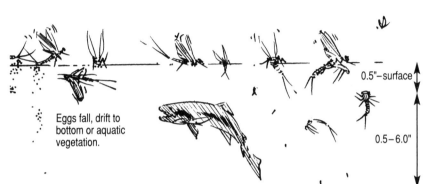

Eggs fall, drift to bottom or aquatic vegetation.

0.5"–surface

0.5–6.0"

Nymphs continue ascent to surface.

TACTICS
1. Dead-drift nymphing. Use two-fly rig with one imitation close to weight. Place point fly 12 or more inches from first fly.
2. Freestyle nymphing. For slower, shallower water or spooky trout.
3. Suspension nymphing. Suspend fly at depth trout are feeding.

FLY PATTERN TYPES
1. Standard nymph with or without flash. Soft hackle.
2. Beadheads.
ACTIVE FEEDING INDICATORS
1. Trout suspended higher up in water.
2. Flashing, darting movements.

Nymphs mature in streambed rubble. Once in a while they get accidentally swept into the drift, but they aren't a common component of behavioral drift.

FLY PATTERN TYPES
1. Standard nymph pattern. Match size, color.
2. Beadhead nymph.
3. Flashback standard nymph pattern.
ACTIVE FEEDING INDICATORS
1. Trout suspended above the streambed.
2. Flashing, darting movement.

Pale morning dun nymphs are moderate swimmers that may drift close to the streambed for a while before ascending with an undulating movement to the surface.

TACTICS
1. **Dead-drift nymphing. Place an imitation closer to weight to imitate naturals drifting close to bottom.**
2. Freestyle nymphing. For slower, shallower water.

 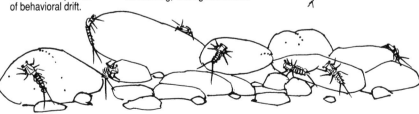

When the nymphs do actually begin to emerge, they release from the bottom and drift downstream for a ways before they begin clumsily swimming to the surface with a pulsating-type movement. During the initial drift they remain close to the bottom. Whether using a two-fly or single-fly rig, make sure that one of the flies is from 6 to 8 inches from the weight. Keeping the weight close to your nymph imitation will keep it in the zone where the trout are looking for naturals. If the trout detect drag in the presentation during this early phase of the emergence, they will likely be repulsed. Use your mending skills to prevent it throughout the drift.

The Front End of the Hatch. Eventually, there will be enough nymphs in the water to pull the trout up closer to the surface. Expect to see bulges, some more energetic boils, and the always challenging head-to-tail rise. If you thought the front end of the blue-winged olive hatch was tough, wait until you come up against the pale morning duns! I've fished hatches where I couldn't buy a strike until the trout switched over from taking front-end-of-the-hatch emergers to feeding predominantly on duns.

I'm still not sure what causes this extreme selectivity, but it might have something to do with the amount of time it takes the pale morning duns to get into the air. My observations are qualitative, but it seems that under typical hatch conditions it takes the duns a little longer to break out of the nymphal shuck once the nymph has arrived at the surface, *and* once the dun does emerge, it takes its wings a little longer to harden than other mayfly species before it can take to the air. It's a period of extreme vulnerability when the trout have plenty of time to scrutinize and then leisurely take the incapacitated emerger of their choice. But there's a paradox—the bulges, boils, and head-to-tail riseforms don't indicate that kind of leisurely pursuit. You'd expect simple rises or sips if the prey was that helpless.

I don't have a definitive answer, but here are some things that have worked for me over the years. When you first begin to see surface activity, it may appear chaotic. If you're seeing mostly bulges and headless head-to-tail rises, try to pick out individual feeding fish. Find the trout with the predictable feeding patterns. Switch to a single unweighted nymph pattern (I always start with a version of the pheasant tail nymph) tied to a long, supple tippet with no strike indicator. Present the fly with a slack-line presentation 1 foot upstream from a regularly feeding trout. A drag-free drift is crucial. If you can't find a trout with a predictable feeding rhythm, locate areas where the feeding is most active, whether it's a single fish or several fish. Cast the fly 2 feet above the area of active feeding and allow it to drift drag-free through the bulges or head-to-tail rises. You'll have less of a chance to hook a fish than you would if you cast to a single, spotted trout, but nonetheless, if the drift is drag-free, there is a chance to hook up.

I stumbled across another quirky tactic when I was fishing to a caddisfly hatch that blended into a pale morning dun hatch. I was on the verge of switching from a standard size 18 bleached Elk Hair Caddis to my pale morning dun floating nymph pattern when I got a strike as the Elk Hair Caddis made an underwater swing at the end of the drift. A few more casts proved that the trout would consistently hit the submerged Elk Hair Caddis on the swing. Since that time I've successfully used the tactic during the front end of the hatch on numerous occasions.

The best explanation I can come up with for the success of this tactic is that I might actually have been fishing to a hatch of pale yellow-bodied duns *other* than *Ephemerella*. Duns of some of these mayflies, such as the pale evening duns (*Heptagenia*), apparently emerge from the nymphal shuck *before* they reach the surface. They ascend with their wings folded back, which would explain why the Elk Hair Caddis silhouette works.

Later I applied the tactic to a real pale morning dun hatch, and it also worked. Who knows why? Some aquatic entomologists think that pale morning duns may sometimes emerge underwater, too. Or maybe the trout simply take the caddis as an attractor pattern that doesn't necessarily imitate the emergence characteristics of the hatch. It could be that the trout just like the color or maybe they like the looks of the pattern fished on the swing. All I can say is give it a try the next time you encounter pale yellow-bodied duns hatching and see if it works for you.

On Top. If you're seeing heads pop up on the surface, switch to a floating nymph. The pheasant tail floating nymph is among my all-time highest-producing fly patterns on the pale morning dun hatch, and it is most effective during the front end of the hatch. My standard drill with the floating nymph is to fish it alone if I can see it. I like to cast it upstream and across when possible. If the trout are really spooky, a downstream cast is often the answer.

If I can't see the floating nymph on the surface, I trail it 12 to 18 inches behind a dun imitation, which I use as a strike indicator. Remember that if you're fishing a dry fly with a floating trailer, it can be more difficult to get a drag-free drift while maintaining separation between the floating nymph and dun once they land on the water. A down-and-across reach cast is an ideal presentation where possible.

During heavier pale morning dun hatches there will often be high numbers of duns that don't successfully make it out of their nymphal shucks and float crippled on the surface. Other duns may emerge but for some reason don't get into the air. If the trout aren't taking a lot of duns from the surface, but are not interested in the floating nymph, a crippled dun imitation fished on or just below the surface may attract strikes.

A soft-hackle pale morning dun imitation is a good representation of a dun that has not made it into the air and has sunk below the surface. The soft-hackle fly should be presented with a slack-line cast to produce a drag-free drift. At times, soft hackles are effective when cast directly to rising fish. Seining the upper 12 inches of the surface will help you determine if there are drowned duns or cripples. Be sure to seine directly downstream from your targeted fish. And finally, if you don't find high numbers of cripples or drowned duns in the drift, don't let that prevent you from fishing their imitations if other emerger-style patterns are ineffective. There are always trout that will feed opportunistically on these vulnerable insects.

The fishing usually gets a little more predictable when the trout switch over to taking duns. In slower-moving water, a dry fly that sits down in the surface film will usually do the trick. In faster-moving riffles, a traditionally hackled pattern will be easier to see. Other than that, a drag-free presentation is often all you need. It should be pointed out, however, that even when the trout are taking duns, they will probably continue to be receptive to unweighted nymphs, floating nymphs, cripple patterns, or soft hackles fished alone or as a trailer behind the dun imitation.

Spinners. When the pale morning duns are on, I'm always surprised to see fly fishers leave the river before the evening spinner fall. I look forward to the spinner fall as some of the best fishing of the hatch. Since the spinner has fallen dead to the water after egg-laying, there is no threat that it can escape from the trout, so expect to see sipping or leisurely simple riseforms. Although the male and female spinners differ in color, I've always done well with the trusty Rusty spinner. An evening spinner fall is the norm on most of the rivers where I fish, but pale morning dun spinner falls can also occur in the morning or for that matter almost any time of the day. It's even possible for a spinner fall from the previous day's hatch to get mixed in with the next day's dun hatch, so be on guard if you see the characteristic leisurely sipping rises of a spinner fall when duns are on the water!

I look for the rises to the spent spinners on the flats below the riffles where the duns hatched. Standard slack-line presentations are required, but you don't usually have to get fancy. In the evening, the low-light conditions will probably make it hard to see an already difficult-to-see spinner imitation on the surface, so you may have to resort to the regular tricks for determining where your fly is. Don't be too worried about whether your fly is floating right up on the surface all the time either. The trout will often take a spent spinner imitation that's submerged a few inches under the surface.

TRICOS

General Information

Nymph: Dark brown to black. Chunky, robust body. Three tails. Poor swimmer.

Dun: Gray/white wings with no hind wing. Three tails. Female has olive body, male's is dark gray. Wings seem oversize in relation to small, robust body.

Spinner: Wings clear. No hind wing. Three long tails. Female has olive body. Male has dark brown/black body.

Size Range: Matches size 20 to 24 hook.

Representative Genera: *Tricorythodes.*

Hatch Times: July to October. Males hatch at twilight. Females hatch at dawn.

Notes: The Tricos are renowned for producing superabundant spinner falls. In rivers where Tricos are well represented, expect the trout to become hyperselective as the season, and the hatch, progresses.

The Real Beginning. Most small-fly aficionados know that the female Tricos hatch very early in the morning and go almost directly into mating swarms. Egg-laying and the subsequent spinner fall can begin as early as 10 A.M. The spinner fall occurs later and later in the day as the hatch progresses into the autumn. Many fly fishers time their arrival on the river for the beginning of the spinner fall. I always make a point to be on the water at dawn. That's when the females hatch, and it may be when you have the best chance to consistently catch trout, especially later in the season.

The female Trico hatch is pretty much your standard meat-and-potatoes mayfly hatch. I've found that in the West where I fish it, I seldom need more than a parachute-style dun imitation that's the right size. Unlike most other small-fly fishers, I do carry a Trico nymph imitation. Although most of the writers I've read report that the nymph imitation has no importance because

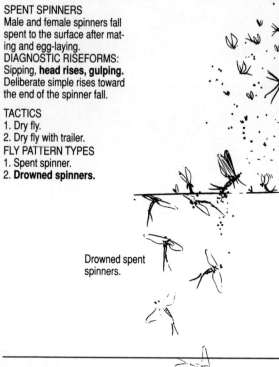

SPENT SPINNERS
Male and female spinners fall spent to the surface after mating and egg-laying.
DIAGNOSTIC RISEFORMS: Sipping, **head rises, gulping.** Deliberate simple rises toward the end of the spinner fall.

TACTICS
1. Dry fly.
2. Dry fly with trailer.
FLY PATTERN TYPES
1. Spent spinner.
2. **Drowned spinners.**

Drowned spent spinners.

Due to the huge number of spent spinners, many more will be available to trout at lower depths.

TACTICS
1. Dead-drift nymphing.
2. Suspension nymphing.
3. Freestyle nymphing in slow, shallow water.
FLY PATTERN TYPES
1. **Weighted drowned spinner.**

Note: Information in boldface type is especially important for this hatch.

Tricos: Matching the Life Cycle

FLY PATTERN TYPES
1. Dry fly.
2. Nymph.
3. Floating nymph.

Mating swarm.

Eggs fall, drift to bottom or aquatic vegetation.

0.5 inch to surface: Nymphs in surface film. They emerge from shucks and get airborne quickly. Female duns molt to spinners almost immediately.
DIAGNOSTIC RISEFORMS: Sipping, simple to complex rises, head-to-tail.

TACTICS
1. **Dry fly.**
2. **Dry fly with trailer.**
3. Greased leader.

0.5"–surface

Nymphs arrive just below the surface.
DIAGNOSTIC RISEFORMS: Bulges, wedges, headless head-to-tail. At times no riseform is visible.

TACTICS
1. Dry fly with trailer.
2. Freestyle nymphing with unweighted imitation or lightly weighted imitation.
3. Greased leader.
FLY PATTERN TYPES
1. Standard mayfly nymph.
2. Beadhead.

0.5–6.0"

ACTIVE FEEDING INDICATORS
1. Trout suspended higher up in the water.
2. An occasional flash. Trout might just suspend and pick off the numerous nymphs.

Female nymphs continue ascent to surface. Fishing to trout at this stage of the hatch can be productive at times.

TACTICS
1. Suspension nymphing.
2. Freestyle nymphing in slower-moving, more shallow water.
3. Dead-drift nymphing. Lengthen the distance between the point fly and the weight.
FLY PATTERN TYPES
1. Standard mayfly nymph pattern.
2. Beadhead nymph.

Trico nymphs aren't typical components of behavioral drift. They remain hidden in silts of slower-moving sections of the river until they hatch.

ACTIVE FEEDING INDICATORS
1. Trout suspended above stream bottom.
2. Occasional flashing.

Female nymphs hatch in early morning. **The initial ascent of the nymphs to the surface has limited value to fly fishers.**

TACTICS
1. Dead-drift nymphing.
2. Freestyle nymphing in slower, shallow water.
FLY PATTERN TYPES
1. Standard mayfly nymph—match size, color.

the hatch occurs too early in the morning, I've found it useful when the trout become selective to the dun imitation later in the season. I simply trail the nymph 15 inches or so behind the dun imitation. I've even trailed nymph imitations behind spent spinner imitations during the spinner fall with good results.

As a rule, the dun hatch doesn't last very long, and there is usually a lull in feeding activity when the males and females fly into the mating swarms over the river. As time passes, the mating swarms will get closer and closer to the water, and then you'll begin to see the first of the females peel out to lay their eggs. It's not long after that when the first of the spinners fall spent on the water.

Spinners. The trout's response to the Trico spinner fall is always a surprise. They come out of nowhere to stack up in the prime feeding lanes, and when the prime lies are full, they'll fill up any trace of current that will carry the spinners to them. The number of spinners always seems way out of proportion to the number of duns that you saw hatching at dawn! And that's actually one of the problems. There can be so many naturals on the water that your well-presented imitation gets no respect.

Look for energetic simple riseforms at first that belie the fact that the spinners are dead and not going away. Look for larger trout to make gulping head rises along prime feeding lies when the spinners begin to stack up. You'll hear the distinctive lip-popping sound of the rise. Before long you may witness trout rising all over the river. Now's the time to calm yourself. Don't start thinking this is going to be easy just because there are so many spinners and so many rising trout. Odds are it won't be. If you let it get to you, you could crack right there on the river. And it's no fun calling in the medics when you come across a fly fisher suffering from Trico shock. . . .

The most important ingredient for success during a full-blown Trico spinner fall is for your fly to drift drag-free over the trout at the right moment of its feeding cycle. You can expect that almost every trout you see, whether it's gulping or sipping, will be locked into a definite feeding rhythm. It will not deviate from that rhythm to take your imitation. Why should it? There are ten million *real* bugs right in front of its nose.

Forget about cleverly timing your cast. The key to the Tricos is to simply make as many accurate casts as you can and hope that one of them coincides with the trout's cycle. Put the fly 8 inches to a foot upstream from the trout—again and again and again. You will risk putting the fish down, but even if you do, it will probably come back in a matter of minutes. If it doesn't, you won't have any trouble finding another one to cast to.

If this all sounds a little tedious, well, sometimes it can be. Trout rising to Trico spinners can be maddeningly difficult to catch. But there are some tricks. Sometimes the fly pattern will make a difference during the Trico spinner fall. Carry several variations that use different wing materials. In addition, carry several patterns that are designed to sink. Remember, the spinners are floating dead on the surface. If the current bumps up against a rock or drops over a ledge, some of the spent spinners will get pushed under the surface.

I learned the value of fishing a drowned Trico spinner when I was fishing my regular Trico spent spinner patterns. Since they were so small and lay down almost invisibly in the surface film, I wasn't surprised that I couldn't see them. I simply employed other methods to detect strikes. One day I got close enough to some rising fish that I thought I would be able to see my imitation on the surface. I actually did, too, but only for about half of my casts. For the other half the fly was sinking below the surface. And those were the drifts where I was getting most of my strikes!

It then occurred to me that the reason I wasn't seeing my fly on many of my presentations was that it was sinking. A Trico spinner imitation doesn't have much to buoy it up in the film. I went back to the fly-tying bench and modified some of my spinner patterns specifically so that they would sink. I now catch as many as 50 percent of my trout on these patterns during the Trico spinner fall! In a pinch, a drowned Trico can be fished as the point fly on a dead-drift nymphing rig, but it's more fun fished either as a single fly or as a trailer behind a dry fly.

If you are having trouble seeing your fly or decide to try drowned Trico spinner patterns, try rigging them as a trailer 12 to 18 inches behind a size 18 or size 16 bleached Elk Hair Caddis. It's easy to see, and surprisingly, everywhere I've ever used the combination for a Trico hatch I end up catching some fish on the caddis imitation! The idea that a fly imitation that doesn't have anything at all to do with the hatch may catch fish isn't a new revelation, either. Small-fly anglers have used size 20 or 22 ant patterns with great success during the Trico spinner hatch for years.

Mike Lawson has been pioneering "unmatching the hatch" tactics for years on the Henry's Fork. He devotes an entire chapter to it in his book *Spring Creeks*. Lawson reasons that when the surface is covered with hundreds of emerging or spent insects, fishing a fly that doesn't match them, such as a tiny Royal Wulff attractor pattern, may capture the trout's attention. I know it works for the Trico spinner fall, where I've had success fishing tiny ants, beetles, and even Renegades.

There are various timing strategies that can change your luck during the Trico hatch, too. If you can, try to fish the spinner fall during the first few weeks after it begins. The trout are usually more aggressive then, and the larger fish haven't figured out yet that they can just lay low and take drowned spinners. Expect the fish to get considerably more selective after those first few weeks. If you can't manage to get on the water when the hatch first starts, try to get on the water right when the spinner fall begins for the day. The trout often feed with a little more abandon at the beginning of the spinner fall.

Also, don't take your spinner imitation off just because you don't see any more spinners in the air or on the water. After the major thrust of the spinner fall is over, there are always lots of

Tying a spent Trico spinner imitation to the tippet with a loop may give it better action.

spent spinners left on the surface. They may be hung up in little back eddies, awash on rocks, or stuck in the grass along the bank. But they often end up back in the current. I pay special attention to the soft water along the banks after the spinner fall. It's not unusual to spot a trout quietly sipping spinners as they trickle downstream along the bank. And these after-the-spinner-fall risers are often larger than average. Even if you don't see rises, consider systematically casting the spent spinner imitation up against grassy banks. You might be surprised.

Finally, if you find yourself in the midst of a huge spinner fall with uncooperative trout rising all around you, consider moving to a location where there are fewer trout rising. I look for slower-moving side currents along the bank that might be feeding a few trout a sporadic supply of spent spinners. These fish may be a bit less picky. If you still can't get them to take, try tying the spinner imitation to your tippet with a tiny surgeon's loop. I've found that the imitation will turn and hinge against the loop when it's drifting downstream in slower currents. I often get a strike right when the fly turns against the loop.

MIDGES

General Information

Larva: Small, key feature is wormlike appearance with a distinct head. No legs. Body segmented. All colors are found, but olive, black, gray, blood red, and dirty white seem most important in trout waters.

Pupa: Slender, segmented abdomen. Large thorax with well-defined wing pads usually visible. Some pupae are active, free-swimmers. Others live in conical or cylindrical cocoons from which they emerge at maturity and swim to the surface. Same colors as seen in larva, although olive, gray, and black seem especially important.

Adult: Two wings. Long, slender abdomen. Long legs. Male may have plumelike antenna. Same colors as pupae. Often actively dance on surface. Adults form mating clusters on water's surface.

Size Range: Matches size 18 to 32 hook.

Representative Families: Chironomidae (includes numerous subfamilies). Simuliidae (not described above, important on some waters).

Hatch Time(s): Hatch throughout the year. Winter, early spring, and late fall are most important to anglers because there are no other hatches at the time.

The Real Beginning. Midges are the graduate course in small–fly fishing. Pursuing trout that are feeding on them is often fraught with contradictions and weirdness. It is wise to never trust what you learn one day to be true the next when it comes to these tiny two–winged flies. When it comes to midges, take it one day at a time. This is truly a fly-fishing master game.

The riddles start with the real beginning of the hatch. Most small–fly anglers will report that they have been successful fishing midge larva imitations, even when a hatch was not imminent. The contradiction is that midge larvae, as a rule,

---

MATING MIDGES
Adults often form mating clusters on the surface where a number of males attempt to mate with a female. At other times a single male and a single female will join in a knotted pair. Trout key on these vulnerable mating midge clusters and pairs.
DIAGNOSTIC RISEFORMS: Active simple to complex riseform, gulps, head rises, occasional splashy rise, sips.

TACTICS
1. Dry fly.
FLY PATTERN TYPES
1. **Midge cluster.**
2. Fore-and-Aft.
3. Palmer-hackle dry fly.

In some species female returns to water to lay eggs. Other species may lay eggs on emergent vegetation.

Midge larvae are a major component of behavioral drift and are available to trout year-round. Dead-drift nymphing a midge larva imitation any time of year is effective where midges are plentiful.

Note: Information in boldface type is especially important for this hatch.

Midges: Matching the Life Cycle

0.5 inch to surface: Pupae in surface film. Some will be vertical, others will be horizontal when actually hatching. Watch for casualities—adults stuck in shuck, stillborns, cripples. Pupae may drift downstream for some distance before they become airborne.

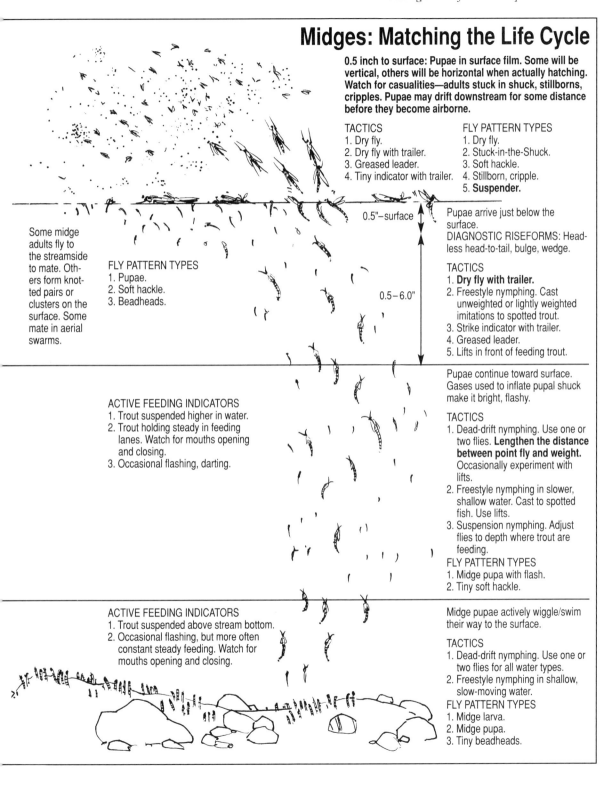

TACTICS
1. Dry fly.
2. Dry fly with trailer.
3. Greased leader.
4. Tiny indicator with trailer.

FLY PATTERN TYPES
1. Dry fly.
2. Stuck-in-the-Shuck.
3. Soft hackle.
4. Stillborn, cripple.
5. **Suspender.**

0.5"–surface

Pupae arrive just below the surface.
DIAGNOSTIC RISEFORMS: Headless head-to-tail, bulge, wedge.

TACTICS
1. **Dry fly with trailer.**
2. Freestyle nymphing. Cast unweighted or lightly weighted imitations to spotted trout.
3. Strike indicator with trailer.
4. Greased leader.
5. Lifts in front of feeding trout.

0.5–6.0"

Some midge adults fly to the streamside to mate. Others form knotted pairs or clusters on the surface. Some mate in aerial swarms.

FLY PATTERN TYPES
1. Pupae.
2. Soft hackle.
3. Beadheads.

ACTIVE FEEDING INDICATORS
1. Trout suspended higher in water.
2. Trout holding steady in feeding lanes. Watch for mouths opening and closing.
3. Occasional flashing, darting.

Pupae continue toward surface. Gases used to inflate pupal shuck make it bright, flashy.

TACTICS
1. Dead-drift nymphing. Use one or two flies. **Lengthen the distance between point fly and weight.** Occasionally experiment with lifts.
2. Freestyle nymphing in slower, shallow water. Cast to spotted fish. Use lifts.
3. Suspension nymphing. Adjust flies to depth where trout are feeding.

FLY PATTERN TYPES
1. Midge pupa with flash.
2. Tiny soft hackle.

ACTIVE FEEDING INDICATORS
1. Trout suspended above stream bottom.
2. Occasional flashing, but more often constant steady feeding. Watch for mouths opening and closing.

Midge pupae actively wiggle/swim their way to the surface.

TACTICS
1. Dead-drift nymphing. Use one or two flies for all water types.
2. Freestyle nymphing in shallow, slow-moving water.

FLY PATTERN TYPES
1. Midge larva.
2. Midge pupa.
3. Tiny beadheads.

shouldn't be readily available to the trout. Most are bottom dwelling, and many species live in tubes in the mud or silt, or they build tiny silk-lined cases that they attach to the stream bottom rubble or aquatic plants.

Nonetheless, on many tailwaters and spring creeks, a midge larva imitation fished using dead-drift nymphing techniques is a good bet anytime there isn't a hatch in progress and sometimes even if there is—no matter what's hatching! The answer to this apparent contradiction is a phenomenon that entomologists call behavioral drift. It turns out that the midge larvae often release themselves into the current and drift downstream. The behavior makes it possible for the species to disperse to areas where there is less competition for food and other necessary resources. Needless to say, the trout take advantage of the larvae's vulnerability when they drift downstream. Angler/entomologist Rick Hafele reports that while behavioral drift occurs 24 hours a day, it peaks from an hour before sunrise until an hour after sunrise and then peaks again from an hour before sunset to an hour after sunset. A third peak occurs after dark. Studies indicate that midge larvae make up the major component of behavioral drift. Other trout food species that also participate in this behavior are blue-winged olive nymphs, some caddisfly species, scuds, and blackfly larvae.

The lesson here is to always trust the midge larva when nothing's going on. I like to dead-drift it in two-fly combinations. I rig a larva imitation closest to the weight so that it stays near the bottom, and then I'll put another similar larva imitation on the point so that I cover two feeding zones. If you're fishing slow, deep water or feel like the action of the fly is inhibited by the leader, consider using the stealth dead-drift rig with 6X tippet material from the strike indicator down to the fly. A fluorocarbon stealth rig is another possibility if the leader is spooking fish, but remember that fluorocarbon is stiffer, so the fly's action could be inhibited.

The other rig I use to present midge larva imitations is a favorite of many tailwater guides. A larger fly, typically a San Juan Worm or general purpose beadhead, is tied in closest to the weight and the larva imitation is tied in as the point fly 12 to 18 inches from the worm. For my money the longer the distance between the two flies the better. This rig is used to search deeper runs and likely looking holding water. It can also be used to fish to trout you spot in deeper water where the weight and strike indicator won't spook them.

The larva imitation also fishes well using freestyle nymphing tactics to trout spotted in slower-moving water, even when there are no apparent hatches. A tiny 1.5mm or 2mm bead will add enough weight to sink the imitation. A fluorocarbon tippet is also helpful. Some of my best days astream have been when I quietly walked the banks on slow days and fished midge larva imitations to trout tucked up against grassy banks.

Also consider using a midge pupa and midge larva combination for two-fly nymphing rigs during nonhatch situations. Although midge pupae are not as common in the drift as larvae, they will still attract strikes, probably because the trout are accustomed to seeing them. I prefer the pupa imitation as the point fly, but it pays to experiment with placement.

On and Near the Top. The importance of the midge pupa imitation will change considerably when you run into a real midge hatch. You'll know something is in the works because the trout begin to assemble in the feeding lanes the same way they do for the mayfly hatches. When you seine the water you'll start coming up with more and more midge pupae. The adults are fully formed inside the pupal shuck at this time and are often quite active. In slower water you'll see them swim up to the surface, hang there in a vertical position, then swim back down a few inches, then back up, and so on until they eventually lie horizontal in the surface film and the adult midge pops into the air.

When the pupae are hanging vertically in the film, you'll notice a little tube that breaks through the surface. It gathers air that helps the adult free itself from its shuck. The nervous swimming back and forth to the surface is a survival tactic. The pupae are incredibly vulnerable at this stage, and the swimming may throw off a few trout.

The trout almost always work a midge hatch in slower-moving water. One reason is that some species of midges hatch from the muddy or silty bottoms typical of slow-moving water. Another one is that it makes more sense from a metabolic point of view to gorge on the plentiful but tiny insects—the fish don't have to use up a lot of calories fighting the current.

During the initial stages of the hatch you may spot trout suspended a foot or two off the bottom furiously picking off pupae as they ascend to the surface. There will usually be more than one fish, and they'll often be suspended at the same level. This is an ideal situation to use a suspension-style nymphing rig. Use either a dry fly or strike indicator to suspend a pupa imitation at the level the trout are feeding.

The thrust of the hatch will eventually work its way up to the surface. Expect to see a variety of riseforms during the hatch. At the beginning, when there are a lot of pupae below the surface, look for gentle bulges and head-to-tail rises. This is a good time to cast single, unweighted soft-hackle pupa imitations. I put the fly within 6 inches of where I think the trout's head is and allow it to dead-drift for a few moments. If I don't get a strike, I sometimes twitch it or lift it a bit. On long, slow flats, let it swing at the end of the drift with the rod tip down near the water. I often feel the strike the same time I see it and set up with just a little strip strike.

It isn't long after the first riseform before you see heads popping up on the surface and a variety of accompanying riseforms. These trout are taking the adults that are struggling to get from their pupal shucks into the air, adults that have

become stuck in their pupal shucks, stillborns, and any pupae still wiggling a few inches below the surface. Or, more simply put, the trout are onto anything they can get their mouths around.

Look for them to be holding just below the surface. You may even see a dorsal fin or the tip of a tail once in a while. The most common riseform will be a gentle sip. During especially heavy hatches, the trout will string sips together with short upstream movements that may even turn into head rises. Mixed in with the sips you'll see underwater head rolls as the trout take a pupa now and then.

It's a situation that cries out for the two-fly rig. At this stage of the hatch I use a dry fly, such as an Adams parachute or small Elk Hair Caddis, that may attract the trout's interest but doesn't necessarily match any adults I see popping out on the surface. That's because even if I see the fish take a few adults, the main action is still going to be to the pupae. The fact is that the main action for the entire hatch will typically be to the pupae, even when the adults on the surface outnumber them. Unlike many mayfly duns, most species of midge adults don't spend a lot of time fooling around on the surface once they work their way out of the shuck. Some pop almost immediately into the air. The trout are more inclined to take the vulnerable pupae that may be stuck in their shucks, stillborn, or crippled than chase down adults, but if an adult happens to skitter over their position, they'll take it as a matter of course.

A key to success during this phase of the midge hatch is to never forget that the trout are holding just under the surface. That limits their window of visibility out of the water, which means that with very careful wakeless wading you should be able to get close to the rising fish. I often get within 10 feet of regularly rising trout. It's best to make a quiet approach from either downstream or downstream and across. When I get to my desired casting position, which hopefully has the sun to my back, I like to wait five or so minutes for things to settle down before I make my first cast. Under the best circumstances, I'll be close enough to see my fly on the surface, make casts where very little or no fly line lands on the water, and control any drag by just lifting the rod tip. Finally, since the trout are finning so close to the surface, I seldom have to put the fly more than 6 inches to a foot upstream of the trout. Sometimes I put the fly right on its nose!

I often target trout that are rising in almost imperceptibly slow-moving ribbons of current near the banks or in backwater sloughs that carry a steady supply of pupae and adults to them. This water is typically quite shallow, and if it's moving over a mud or silt bottom, it's not uncommon to see a fish tailing as it picks off pupae as they leave their tubes in the mud. The trout are more sensitive to surface disruptions in the slow water, so I usually switch back to a single fly. In large backwaters or sloughs, the fishing closely resembles stillwater situations where the trout cruise, looking for pupae and adults. This is a situation where I've had consistent success fishing tiny adult imitations. I try to cast them within 6 inches of the sipping trout. If there's a little wind, I like to use an active dry fly, such as a Fore-and-Aft pattern, that tumbles and skates over the surface.

Much like the Trico spinner fall, success during the midge hatch requires making a lot of accurate casts for every fish hooked and brought to net. It's easy to get sucked into the one pattern, one trout syndrome when the going gets tough. It occurs when you switch flies and soon there-

Slow-moving backwaters can provide excellent small-fly fishing opportunities when the midges are on.

after get a strike and hookup and land the fish. After that initial fish, you then go strikeless, switch flies again, and the same thing happens. If you're not careful, you find yourself switching flies every few casts. All I can say is keep it in perspective. If changing flies is what you have to do to catch fish, it's what you have to do. But oftentimes you'll get a few more strikes per fly if you work on the presentation or simply move upstream or downstream a few feet to change the drift. There's seldom a silver bullet fly during a midge hatch, and you can waste a lot of good fishing time if you're changing flies too often.

Clusters. Sometimes just when things are beginning to seem hopeless you are saved by clusters of mating midges. I've seen some as big as golf balls on New Mexico's San Juan River,

but more commonly they go anywhere from five or six insects to the size of a small grape. The trout will sometimes drop their guard a bit when the clusters appear and you can catch them on a Griffith's Gnat or similar palmer-hackle imitation. More than anything, midge clusters on the water are a relief because you can actually *see* your fly out there. And seeing the fly on the water always means more successful hookups.

Midges in Winter. Some of the best midging occurs on tailwaters and spring creeks during the winter months. Unlike most other aquatic insects, the midges hatch year-round. Feeding activity to the midges in the cold months can be surprisingly heavy. Tactics for winter midging are pretty much the same as those used at other

Some of the best midging occurs during the winter months.

times of the year, but there are some cold-weather equipment considerations.

Aside from the obvious extra layers of clothing needed for winter outdoor activities, you may want to consider boot-foot waders if you plan to do a lot of winter midging. They'll keep your feet warmer. Some hard-core winter midgers carry two rods—one rigged for dead-drift nymphing and the other rigged for dry flies—to avoid freezing their hands rerigging a single rod when the trout switch from subsurface to surface feeding.

On especially cold days, expect water to freeze in the rod's line guides. It can be broken out by hand or momentarily removed by swishing the rod under the water. If your hands are cold, be especially careful when breaking ice from the guides. Place the rod on the ground and work your way up to the tip-top guide, breaking the ice out of each guide as you go. Avoid holding the rod under your arm and bending the tip toward you to break the ice out of the tip-top guide. It's very easy to break the tip by bending it too much when your hands are cold and lack sensitivity.

Finally, fish during the prime-time winter hours of 10 A.M. to 3 P.M. It's not necessary to be on the water at dawn. Most of the time, hatches will taper off in the afternoon, but I have occasionally fished to dimpling trout until dark during the winter.

Blackflies (*Simuliidae* spp.). Blackfly larvae and pupae are important on some tailwaters and spring creeks. If you are familiar with British fly-fishing literature you will know that *Simuliidae* spp. are the famous reed or riffle smuts where the term "smutting" rise came from. American small-fly anglers use "sipping," "dimpling," and, to a lesser degree, "smutting" to describe the riseform seen when trout are taking midge pupae (or blackfly pupae) in slow-moving waters.

My experience with tiny blackflies is limited to dead-drift nymphing larva imitations in the lower section of the South Platte River. The larvae, which have a distinctive swelling toward the rear of the abdomen, typically attach themselves by it to rocks or other objects in moderately flowing waters with their heads facing downstream. On some tailwaters where dense populations of blackflies occur, it's not uncommon to see trout picking them off from the rocks or dislodging them into the drift and eating them.

The blackfly larvae are known at times to hang in the current by a silken thread attached to a rock, vegetation, or other submerged debris. This behavior has led some small-fly anglers to fish larva imitations downstream on a tight, fine tippet. The artificial is allowed to hang in the current to imitate the natural's behavior. Although I have never tried this technique, my friends report some success with it.

Trout also rise to emerging pupae and adults. There are even a few patterns tied specifically to imitate the pupae, but by all accounts, you can get by fishing midge pupa or adult imitations with standard midge tactics if you ever encounter real smutting rises.

MICROCADDIS

General Information

Larva: Long, caterpillar-like. Segmented body. Usually six well-developed thoracic legs. The first four instars are free-swimming. The fifth instar larvae build cases. Head black; body olive, tan important.

Pupa: Remain in sealed purse-shaped cocoon until just before adult emergence. Holds wings tightly against body. Very long antenna.

Adult: Mothlike. Wings mottled dark brown, gray to tan. Body gray, olive-brown. No tail.

Size Range: Match size 20 to 24 hook.

Representative Genera: *Agraylea, Hydroptila, Leucotrichia.*

Hatch Time(s): Most concentrated June to September. May hatch any time of day.

Notes: There are numerous smaller-size caddisflies. In most cases their hatches can be fished successfully with the same tactics used for larger caddisflies. I've stuck to Gary LaFontaine's definition of true microcaddis here, which only contained members of the family Hydroptilidae. The larvae are unique because they don't construct any kind of case until late in their development. The adult females crawl or dive under the surface to lay their eggs.

The Real Beginning. I'm always surprised by the number of little black-headed, olive-bodied microcaddis larvae that I seine out of the South Platte River during the early season. All of those pupae apparently hatch into the dark-winged adults that are plentiful for several weeks toward the end of July.

It always gets my attention when I consistently seine the same insect from the river over an extended period of time. I figure if I'm seeing the insect, so are the trout. The little free-swimming microcaddis larva is especially intriguing because it's probably out there moving around, which makes it available to the trout once in a

Females dive under surface to lay eggs.

TACTICS
1. **Swing gang of flies. Lifts.**
2. Dead-drift nymphing. Lengthen distance between weight and point fly. Swing or lift at end of drift.
3. Classic down-and-across wet-fly presentation. Mend and swing.

FLY PATTERN TYPES
1. LaFontaine Diving Caddis.
2. Soft hackle.

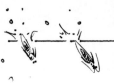

ACTIVE FEEDING INDICATORS
1. Often no signs.
2. Occasionally flashes.
3. Infrequently subtle swirls.

The first four larvae instars are free-swimming. Some of these larvae become available to the trout. Microcaddis larvae may also make up a component of behavioral drift in some waters.

The fifth instar larvae build cases.

Note: Information in boldface type is especially important for this hatch.

Microcaddis: Matching the Life Cycle

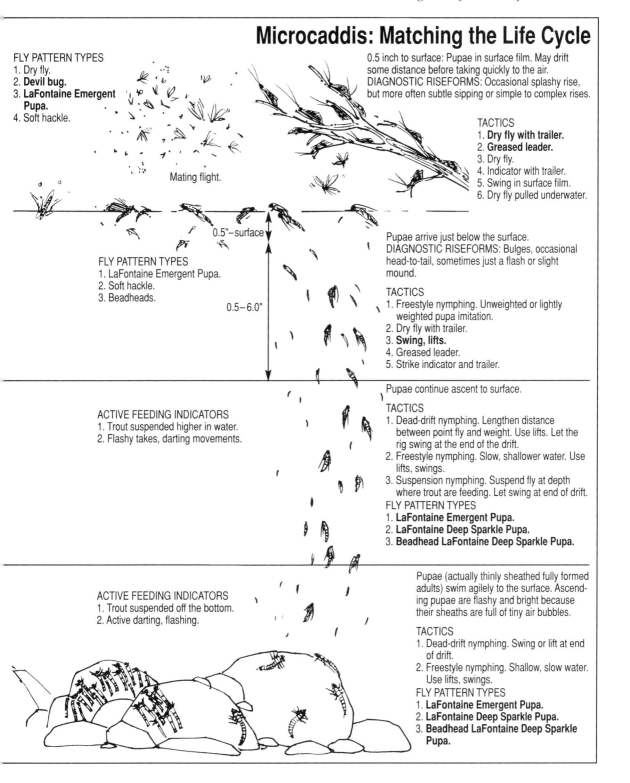

FLY PATTERN TYPES
1. Dry fly.
2. **Devil bug.**
3. **LaFontaine Emergent Pupa.**
4. Soft hackle.

Mating flight.

0.5 inch to surface: Pupae in surface film. May drift some distance before taking quickly to the air.
DIAGNOSTIC RISEFORMS: Occasional splashy rise, but more often subtle sipping or simple to complex rises.

TACTICS
1. **Dry fly with trailer.**
2. **Greased leader.**
3. Dry fly.
4. Indicator with trailer.
5. Swing in surface film.
6. Dry fly pulled underwater.

0.5"–surface

FLY PATTERN TYPES
1. LaFontaine Emergent Pupa.
2. Soft hackle.
3. Beadheads.

0.5–6.0"

Pupae arrive just below the surface.
DIAGNOSTIC RISEFORMS: Bulges, occasional head-to-tail, sometimes just a flash or slight mound.

TACTICS
1. Freestyle nymphing. Unweighted or lightly weighted pupa imitation.
2. Dry fly with trailer.
3. **Swing, lifts.**
4. Greased leader.
5. Strike indicator and trailer.

ACTIVE FEEDING INDICATORS
1. Trout suspended higher in water.
2. Flashy takes, darting movements.

Pupae continue ascent to surface.

TACTICS
1. Dead-drift nymphing. Lengthen distance between point fly and weight. Use lifts. Let the rig swing at the end of the drift.
2. Freestyle nymphing. Slow, shallower water. Use lifts, swings.
3. Suspension nymphing. Suspend fly at depth where trout are feeding. Let swing at end of drift.

FLY PATTERN TYPES
1. **LaFontaine Emergent Pupa.**
2. **LaFontaine Deep Sparkle Pupa.**
3. **Beadhead LaFontaine Deep Sparkle Pupa.**

ACTIVE FEEDING INDICATORS
1. Trout suspended off the bottom.
2. Active darting, flashing.

Pupae (actually thinly sheathed fully formed adults) swim agilely to the surface. Ascending pupae are flashy and bright because their sheaths are full of tiny air bubbles.

TACTICS
1. Dead-drift nymphing. Swing or lift at end of drift.
2. Freestyle nymphing. Shallow, slow water. Use lifts, swings.

FLY PATTERN TYPES
1. **LaFontaine Emergent Pupa.**
2. **LaFontaine Deep Sparkle Pupa.**
3. **Beadhead LaFontaine Deep Sparkle Pupa.**

while. Over the years I've used an imitation of the larva very much the way I use a midge larva. I dead-drift it closest to the weight when I don't see much activity because I know it's plentiful near the stream bottom and familiar to the fish. I often fish it in a two-fly rig with a midge larva or pupa imitation. So, once again, like the midge larva, here's another fly imitation that's effective when there's no apparent hatch.

Things begin to change when the microcaddis pupae are mature, and the thinly sheathed adults, known as pharate adults, swim to the surface. The only way to be sure that the initial subsurface feeding is to microcaddis pupae and not midge pupae is to seine the water. If they are indeed microcaddis, a tiny LaFontaine Deep Sparkle Pupa weighted with a 2mm bead tied close to the weight on the leader and a LaFontaine Emergent Sparkle Pupa on the point of a two-fly dead-drift nymphing rig can be quite effective. Start with a dead-drift presentation, but be sure to allow the flies to swing at the end of the drift.

If you begin picking up strikes at the end of the drift, incorporate that into your presentation. An alternative is to remove the strike indicator and cast the flies down- and across stream, making sure to mend the line as soon as the flies sink. After the mend, allow the flies to swing. You won't have any trouble detecting a strike on the swing.

As more and more pupae ascend, you'll begin to see riseforms. But if you're looking for the familiar splashy rise of a trout chasing down a larger caddisfly pupa or adult, forget it. I've been fooled more than once into thinking that the gentle sipping rises I was seeing in the slow-moving water up against the bank were trout taking midge pupae, only find out that they were actually taking microcaddis pupae. Once again, seining will tell you for sure what the trout are taking, but you might also see some adult caddis-

flies in the air. I emphasize *might* here. I've witnessed some microcaddis hatches where for the life of me I never detected an adult on the water. I suspect that the adults may emerge near the grassy banks and clamber up out of the water onto the bank.

If I do find the trout feeding on or near the top, a two-fly rig works well. I use a Micro Devil Bug as the dry fly and trail a LaFontaine Emergent Sparkle Pupa behind it. Sometimes the Micro Devil Bug is just as effective by itself. If the trout are a little more selective, I've had good success casting the Deep Sparkle Pupa down and across and fishing it on the swing or casting the unweighted Emergent Sparkle Pupa at rises. In tailwaters where I can find moderate riffles, I sometimes make a slack-line cast either across stream or slightly down- and across stream and dead-drift an emergent pupa imitation downstream toward a feeding fish. When the fly is a few feet above the trout, I gently lift the rod tip to simulate an ascending pupa. At other times I'll fish the pupa on a short dead-drift and then twitch it a bit when it's near the trout.

I also carry several styles of adult downwing-style caddis imitations. I have used them with good effect at times, but I usually stick with the pupa unless I see the trout actively taking adults. I make a point to fish adult patterns on the dead drift, with occasional twitching action, and on the swing. If the trout target a specific presentation style, I emphasize it.

One of my favorite fly-fishing revelations occurred when I was fishing to what I thought was a microcaddisfly hatch. I could see a few adults in the air and an occasional boil or even a splashy rise to them. Naturally, I switched to a tiny Elk Hair Caddis, which had absolutely no effect on the trout until, as I related in my book *Tying Small Flies,* I inadvertently allowed the fly to swing after the drift and got a strike. I incorporated a swing into my presentation after that

Three-Fly Diving Microcaddis Rig

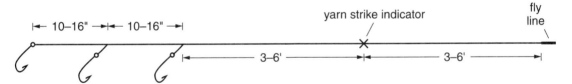

Use classic down-and-across wet-fly presentation, and mend the line to keep flies from swinging too severely.

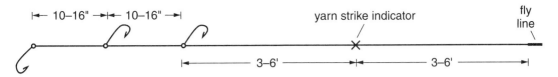

If flies tangle too much using a dropper rig, use an inline rig with flies tied in at the hook eyes.
Note: The three-fly rig works best without weight on the leader. If you need to get the rig down, try attaching weight above the first fly. Cast this rig upstream, and then lift and swing at the end of the drift.

and managed another strike or two, but for the most part got skunked. When I waded out of the river I noticed much to my surprise that my waders were crawling with hundreds of adult caddisflies.

At the time I didn't know that some female caddisflies dive under the surface to lay their eggs. It took a little research when I got home before I realized that the caddisflies on my waders had been diving females. My friend Gary LaFontaine recommended that I match the naturals with his diving caddis imitation and then fish them in a gang of three using classic down-and-across wet-fly tactics to swing the flies in the current. He told me to carefully throw in a mend so that the flies wouldn't swing too severely. This also makes them present broadside to the trout, which results in more strikes. I practiced the tactic for a season and improved my success on this difficult hatch. I now look forward to seeing my waders crawling with the little caddisflies.

Microterrestrials

Never underestimate the power of a tiny ant or beetle to attract a trout's attention. As a rule, I fish micro-ants and beetles the same way I fish larger versions of them. But there are a few things to watch out for. First, don't be fooled into thinking that every sipping rise in slow water is to midges. I once fished a midge pupa imitation to sipping trout on Pennsylvania's Yellow Breeches Creek for three hours before I seined the water and discovered the trout were taking size 22 ants! As usual, the lesson was that you can never go wrong taking a few minutes to seine the river.

I carry floating and sinking small ant and beetle patterns. On the floating ant versions I either trim the hackle or tie a parachute hackle so that the fly sits flush in the surface film. You should have ants in black, brown, cinnamon, and an outrageous hot fluorescent orange or red. I don't know why, but sometimes all it takes to catch a trout during the most difficult midge hatch you've ever experienced is to cast a hot orange ant at them! In contrast, my only tiny beetle imitations are basic black or black with iridescent green.

Although the trout are occasionally selective to a locally plentiful ant or beetle species, I employ ant and beetle patterns mostly to search along the banks or in calmer backwaters or any other place that I think a trout might be lurking near the surface. Over the years, probing the river with an ant pattern has become one of my favorite pastimes when nothing is hatching. I use much the same strategy as I use when I fish a small stream in the high country. I put a cast or two to any place I think there might be a trout. If I'm casting up against grassy banks, I try to land the fly just up on the grass and pull it down into the water. Detecting strikes is usually easy, although occasionally a quite large trout up close against the bank may take a beetle or ant with an incredibly subtle sipping rise.

You may find that sinking versions of these terrestrials are more productive. You'll have to concentrate a bit harder to detect a strike to a fly you can't see, but most of the time it's hard to see a floating ant on the surface, too.

A final tactic for the mighty mini-ants and beetles is to use them during a hatch when nothing else works. I can't count the number of times that an ant or beetle imitation has saved my day during a tough midge hatch or Trico spinner fall. I actually stick an ant imitation to the wool drying patch on my fishing vest during the Trico season to remind me to use it. It sure beats sitting on the bank and scratching my head!

Microscuds

Small-fly fishermen are becoming increasingly aware of microscuds in hook size 18 to 22 in both tailwaters and spring creeks. At first I thought the tiny scud patterns were just another gimmick until I fished my larger scuds side-by-side with a pal who fished his size 20 micros. He cleaned my clock. I'm now a believer.

I fish the microscuds in much the same way I fish midge larvae—more as a general purpose attractor than a match to any special occurrence of scuds. The microscud is effective in two-fly dead-drift nymphing rigs in both positions. I carry weighted and unweighted versions, which I use almost interchangeably in a dead-drift nymphing rig. Sometimes one will produce better than the other, probably because they have different actions in the water.

I like to fish a weighted microscud using freestyle nymphing methods when I hunt larger trout tucked up against the banks. This is sight-fishing at its best that requires me to use all of my small-fly skills. The microscud is a good fly for the job because the trout are used to seeing it show up in the drift throughout much of the season, and it's a high-priority food item for an opportunistically feeding trout. I've actually had a few of the big boys come out from under a cut bank to take the scud.

Fishing a tiny weighted fly in slower water takes some getting used to. As always, get close to the trout. For bankers I approach from downstream, stay low and out of the water whenever possible. The trick is to make the cast far enough upstream of the fish to not spook it when the weighted fly hits the water, but not so far upstream that the imitation gets hung up on the bottom before it drifts down to the fish. When possible, I cast the imitation up on the bank and pull it into the water, which causes very little disruption and lessens the chance that I'll spook the trout. Once the cast is completed and the fly is drifting downstream to the fish, the key is to lift the rod tip and swim it to the trout. If you've managed to get close enough to the fish, you will have only the leader in the water during the drift. That will make it easier to guide the fly.

I love that kind of fishing!

Over the years I've made a point of taking careful notes on small-fly hatches and how the trout respond to them. At first I did it because I was new to guiding and I wanted to have a base of information that I could apply to the next season. I still record what I see because I've found that a year never goes by where I don't notice something new. There are now more than twenty little black notebooks lined up on the bookshelf over my desk. I like to think that I've stored the essence of much of the information contained in those notebooks in my mind and that it helps me make the oddball connections and off-the-wall conclusions that sometimes make the difference during an especially difficult hatch. More than anything, the notebooks have taught me to always keep my eyes open and stay alert on the river, because if they prove anything, it's that there is something new just waiting to be learned. . . .

CHAPTER EIGHT

The Elements of Style

The Trico spinner fall tapered off and finally came to an end hours ago. I like the excitement and the challenge of trying to convince the rising trout to take my spent spinner imitations this late in the summer. It's difficult small-fly fishing, but if you stay focused, landing four or five nice fish is not out of the question.

I especially like this time of year on the South Platte River. Most fly fishers would say there's nothing going on right now, and it's true if you're inside the regulation, high-speed, high-excitement fly-fishing box—no rises, not a lot of trout stacked up in the feeding lanes, no insects in the air. There's just four or five fishermen left on the river. I saw the dust plumes from the trucks of the other ones when they peeled out of the parking lot an hour or so after the Tricos went off. The guides have probably taken their guests down to fish in Elevenmile Canyon, and the recreational fly fishers are either heading home or spreading out over South Park.

The fishermen I can see are all dead-drift nymphing in the usual places. I know that because I've guided this water for more than a decade, and there are about eleven places where the current, water depth, and stream bottom topography come together perfectly to provide ideal holding water. You can always figure there will be trout in these places. There are trout elsewhere in the river, but the numbers game is in your favor at the eleven

places. You find singles, doubles, and the occasional triple everywhere else.

My great pleasure is fishing to the everywhere-else trout. I've come to the river with a single box of tiny flies, a couple of spools of light tippet material, polarized sunglasses, an 8-foot Homer Jennings bamboo fly rod, waders, and a release tool. That's all. It has taken me a long time to learn that this is all I need and even longer to realize it's all I want.

More than anything, I like haunting the banks, stalking trout. Well before I get anywhere close to the river, I check my equipment. Are the leader and tippet in order? Is the rod joined properly? Is the fly line spooled uniformly onto the reel? Sunglasses? I'm tempted to tie a weighted microscud pattern to the end of the tippet because it has produced well for me over the past few seasons, but as is always my habit, I refrain. I'll wait to see what the river tells me.

As I move closer to the water, I maneuver to get the sun at my back and involuntarily crouch down a little. When I'm a little closer, I stop and take a long look at the water. There is a meandering series of bends that cut under the bank, straighten, turn, and then cut under another bank. A hill protects the water from the breeze here, and it's gliding flat with a little riffle here or there. My instinct is to creep down to the river and make a cast up against the bank to just where the current begins to cut under along the bend. But I know I should watch all of this for as long as I can stand it.

Farther up the bank the sky's reflection on the still water deflects briefly. This could be just a wisp of a breeze. Or it could be a trout's signature. The water settles and a few minutes later deflects again. It's no breeze. I sneak closer for a better look. It is a nice brown trout. I back out of sight again, sit down in the grass, and open my fly box. There are dry flies, emergers, and nymph imitations to cover the pale morning duns and blue-winged olives, along with Trico spent spinners, duns, and nymphs. I also have various microcaddis imitations and some never-to-be-without Parachute Adams, little ants, and beetles; midge adult, larva, and pupa patterns, microscuds. . . .

I'm already ahead of the game. I'm thinking that since the trout is a banker I'll want to gently cast whatever fly I choose up on to the grassy bank and pull it into the water. A terrestrial is the obvious choice, but then there were Trico spinners earlier this morning. I finally decide on a size 18 black ant. This particular pattern will ride flush in the surface film. It might even sink after a few casts. I knot it onto the end of the tippet.

I carefully mark the trout's location and then cross the river well downstream from it. I've picked a casting position directly downstream from the trout. It's close, but not close enough that I'll spook the fish getting to it. I crouch low as I work up the bank and then slide quietly down into the water. "Not one ripple," I tell myself.

I'm there, ready, and in position. I strip the fly line I'm going to need from the reel and carefully lay it on the water near where I am now kneeling. I then work out an across-the-body false cast. I'm going to sidearm it to keep the trout from seeing the line and then overpower the cast just enough to get a right-hand curve that will put the fly in the grass two feet upstream from the trout. Then I'll twitch it into the water. . . .

Before I cast I steal a page from the professional athlete's notebook. In my mind I visualize exactly how I want this cast to play out. I know that if I'm very lucky I'll get two or three shots max at this fish, but most likely there will be just this one. The first cast has got to have all the juju. That's what the visualization is about. Once the cast is up in the air, the only thing I want there to be in the world is my concentration on the exact spot where the fly must land.

It's show time. . . . For a moment I feel my cast tug the fly line against the rod's line guides. Then it's just me, the trout, and a spot on the water. I watch, I wait. It seems like forever. And then I see the fly float gently down out of the air and land on target. For less than an instant I think, How can this be? Did I actually do that? But there is no time to contemplate philosophy or magic or the rewards of hard work. A trout is on the move. . . .

As much as I seek out new small-fly patterns, and as much as I've said about how to fish them, I must also say that I have come to believe that fishing small flies is ultimately about having as little as possible between me and the trout. It's fly fishing reduced to its most basic elements. For me, that means going light. But there's a paradox. I don't think I could have gotten to this point without the weight of everything that came before it.

I needed those years where I imitated every size, every shade of color, every life stage, every nuance of a blue-winged olive's, pale morning dun's, Trico's, midge's, or microcaddis's life, before I could understand that sometimes it's as much in the cast as in the imitation. In the end, maybe tying and fishing all those thousands of match-the-hatch imitations wasn't as important as the detailed observations I had to make to come up with the fly. I now know that every hatch has its own quirks. I fish a midge hatch a little differently from a blue-winged olive hatch, but in a pinch, I've also applied some tricks I've learned about trout taking olives to a difficult fish rising to midges.

THE ZONE

My technical fly-fishing pals get a little edgy when I start talking about how the best fly fishing goes beyond the right fly, the right approach, the right casting position, the right cast, the right drift, and the right hookup. But I see them gingerly stepping into the intuitive realm all the time. One pal quietly explained to me that sometimes, when the fishing is tough, he purposely starts fooling around with the fly line when he's dead-drift nymphing. He "pretends" he has "sort of a backlash or something," but at the same time he's still "kinda concentrating" on the strike indicator. He swears he gets more strikes when his attention is deflected in this way.

He emphatically states that he doesn't do "the backlash thing" that often—"only when there's nothing going on." I tell him it's okay with me. What's interesting to me is that he's systematized the ritual to the point that it's a minor tactic. It sounds about as effective as rubbing a worry stone, but it works for him. He was really surprised when I told him that I've been doing something similar for twenty years!

This same sort of thing occurs when someone in your fishing group has the hot hand. No matter what he does, he's catching fish. It might be that you aren't doing squat, so the hot hand gives you his spot on the river and goes to where you weren't catching anything—and he starts catching fish! Meanwhile, you don't get a strike in his spot. Then he gives you the same fly he's using, but the results are still the same—he's hot and you're not. Finally he gives you his rod, fly, and spot, and it still doesn't make any difference. And it could all turn around the next day so that you have the hot hand.

I've fished with the same group of men for close to thirty years. We've often sat around the campfire and talked about how we're all at about the same skill level, but the hot hand thing still seems to happen on close to every trip. The funny thing is that it always seems to even out by the end of the trip. Everybody has the hot hand sooner or later. There even seems to be an equation for big fish, too. Sometimes everybody will be catching trout with the exception of one guy, but at the end of the day he'll catch an exceptionally large fish that makes up for all the small ones he didn't catch.

Most fly fishers take these kinds of experiences as simple coincidence, and it's perfectly possible to fish a lifetime without ever thinking about this kind of off-the-wall stuff. I never did until I got hooked on fishing small flies. But small flies put you so close to the edge that it's difficult to avoid a little of the hocus-pocus. It begins with the fact that small flies are often difficult or impossible to see on the water. When I first started fishing them I very logically used area fishing tactics—if I saw a rise in a predetermined area around where I figured the fly to be, I set the hook.

After several years I began to realize that I wasn't using the area anymore, but rather just setting the hook for reasons that I wasn't exactly sure of. Of course, what I'd done was internalize the area method to the point that I didn't have to consciously think about it every time I presented the fly. The kind of internalization that comes from constant repetitive practice of the same or similar tasks is how angling instinct and intuition are developed.

The same kind of internal knowledge develops when you nymph-fish a lot. You eventually find yourself just setting the hook. If asked exactly *why* you set the hook when you did, you might very well be at a loss for the reason. But rest assured that some part of your mind had registered and acted on all the cues indicative of a strike that you had worked so hard to consciously develop when you were learning to nymph.

When I learned to dead-drift nymph-fish we didn't use strike indicators. Most of us relied on a subtle variety of cues to detect strikes. Although I started off watching the leader/water intersection as a strike indicator, I realized after several years that I was also watching the trout. If I couldn't see the trout, I was watching for any subtle movements in the water that indicated that a trout had moved in any way. At the same time, I was also feeling the fly line for any sense of the quiet electricity that indicates a strike. It occurred to me later that these cues were often more important than the leader/water intersection. When strike indicators became all the rage, I found that I was still using these older, more subtle indicators *and* the strike indicator. That's why I urge beginning nymphers to fish without a strike indicator for a while just so they'll have a chance to develop the more subtle skills.

The same sort of edge develops when you fish very small flies on or near the surface. Since you can't see the fly itself, you learn to react to the trout. Maybe you see just a little dimple where you believe your fly is. Or maybe the light on the surface changes in an odd way. Or maybe some bit of information goes in your eyes and straight to your arm—and you set the hook. You may find that you have a fish on and don't know why!

The presentation used most often when fishing small flies also enhances these intuitive skills. Most small-fly fishers get as close as they can to the trout and make a lot more casts on average before they get a strike. This repetitious casting at short distances still requires full concentration because accuracy is the name of the game in small-fly fishing. The casting almost becomes a meditative state. Or if you're lucky it will—that meditative state will enhance your accuracy. You end up totally in the present; time ceases to exist; and the fly, fly line, and rod simply become an extension of your body . . . and ultimately your will. You've entered the Zone. The Force is with you. It sounds like sci-fi, but if you've fished small flies on a regular basis over the years, I bet you can relate.

I think you can develop these intuitive skills. They may not be among your everyday small-fly tactics, but something extra held in reserve. It will be a frame of mind more than a tactic—a way to utilize more of the information that's out there when things get tough.

First, your fundamentals must be sound. The most common deficit is casting. You must be able to make the necessary casts. At first you will consciously have to analyze each situation and determine if you need a curve cast or a parachute cast or a reach cast. Eventually you will find that you simply apply the right cast or combination of casts without thinking. Good casting takes practice. It really helps to get out on the lawn and just work on your casts. This doesn't mean go down to the park and see how far you can cast. It means practicing your fishing casts—the slack-line stuff, the curves, the reach casts, and the accuracy. Put targets out and work to where you can hit them consistently. When things are slow on the river, take some time to practice your casts on the water. See how a parachute cast works on various types of current. Experiment with an across-body cast. Fool around with a down-and-across reach cast.

One of the difficulties with most casting instruction today is that it's oriented to casting-pond tricks. An average instructor can teach you loop fundamentals, how to improve your distance and accuracy, and the fundamentals of slack-line casts on the lawn or a stillwater casting pond. Learning these fundamentals from a casting pro will indeed speed your learning curve, but once you feel comfortable with the basics, consider engaging an instructor who specializes in fishing casts. Most likely that instructor will be a good guide who's willing to spend a little time with you on the lawn and then takes you to the river. I think it's crucial to learn the fundamentals and then apply those basics to real fishing situations.

THE ELEMENTS OF STYLE

For many years I thought fishing small flies was all about casting the right fly. I thought the right fly pattern was a silver bullet that would solve all my problems. Of course, it didn't. Now I think the answer includes the fly pattern, but also how that pattern is used. I've learned that, with small flies, it often comes down to just matching the size of what the trout are eating and then presenting it in a way that matches, or more accurately doesn't disrupt, their feeding behavior. You must get the fly to where the trout expects it to be and manipulate it in a way that doesn't look unusual to the trout. Needless to say, a perfect match of the natural won't hurt you, but you really do have to get it to where the trout is looking for it. There is a kind of match-the-hatch mythology among small-fly fishers that can be counterproductive if you don't include presentation. Don't fall into the trap.

Fishing small flies should be concise. Don't waste any motion. Include just the necessary elements. Think of it like a drawing. You wouldn't want to see any unnecessary lines, would you? Or consider it as a machine. I'd wonder about a machine that included unnecessary parts. Reduce everything to the basics. Determine what you need for where you fish, know how to use it, have confidence in it, and leave the rest in the truck. For years I carried a vest full of fly boxes, doodads, and gizmos. After a while I started leaving some of the fly boxes that I thought I wouldn't need in the truck. I reasoned that if I ended up really wanting them I could just walk back to the parking area, which was never that far away, and get them. Over time I found myself leaving more and more stuff in the truck. And I have never returned to get any of it.

Reducing the stuff will give you the freedom to concentrate on the trout, or more precisely, the prey. Small-fly angling at its best is trout stalking and trout hunting. You would do well to think of yourself as a predator. Go light, lay low, get small, follow your instinct, and temper your fly fishing with artistry.

Put as little as you can between the trout and yourself.

Arbona, Fred L. Jr. *Mayflies, the Angler, and the Trout.* Tulsa, OK: Winchester Press, 1980.

Borger, Gary A. *Naturals.* Harrisburg, PA: Stackpole Books, 1980.

Clarke, Brian, and John Goddard. *The Trout and the Fly.* New York: Lyons & Burford, 1980.

Engle, Ed. *Fly Fishing the Tailwaters.* Mechanicsburg, PA: Stackpole Books, 1991.

Engle, Ed. *Tying Small Flies.* Mechanicsburg, PA: Stackpole Books, 2004.

Hill, Roger. *Fly Fishing the South Platte River.* Boulder, CO: Pruett Publishing Co., 1991.

Holbrook, Don, and Ed Koch. *Midge Magic.* Mechanicsburg, PA: Stackpole Books, 2001.

Humphreys, Joe. *Trout Tactics.* Harrisburg, PA: Stackpole Books, 1981.

Knopp, Malcom, and Robert Cormier. *Mayflies.* Helena, MT: Greycliff Publishing Co., 1997.

Koch, Ed. *Fishing the Midge.* Harrisburg, PA: Stackpole Books, 1988.

LaFontaine, Gary. *Caddisflies.* Tulsa, OK: Winchester Press, 1981.

Lawson, Mike. *Spring Creeks.* Mechanicsburg, PA: Stackpole Books, 2003.

Marinaro, Vincent C. *A Modern Dry Fly Code.* New York: G. P. Putnam's Sons, 1950.

Marinaro, Vincent C. *In the Ring of the Rise.* Guilford, CT: Globe Pequot Press, 1976.

Martin, Darrel. *Micropatterns, Tying and Fishing the Small Fly.* New York: Lyons & Burford, 1994.

Schwiebert, Ernest. *Trout.* New York: E. P. Dutton, 1978.

Streeks, Neale. *Small Fly Adventures in the West.* Boulder, CO: Pruett Publishing Co., 1996.

Swisher, Doug, and Carl Richards. *Fly Fishing Strategy.* New York: Crown Publishers, 1975.

Swisher, Doug, and Carl Richards. *Selective Trout.* New York: Crown Publishers, 1971.

INDEX

Page numbers in italics indicate illustrations.